OPPOSING
VIEWPOINTS®
SERIES

Interventions

Other Books of Related Interest:

Opposing Viewpoints Series

Behavioral Disorders
Debt
Teen Drug Abuse

Current Controversies Series

Drug Legalization
Medical Ethics
Medical Marijuana

At Issue Series

Are Americans Overmedicated?
Are Privacy Rights Violated?
Do Abstinence Programs Work?

"Congress shall make no law ... abridging the freedom of speech, or of the press."

First Amendment to the US Constitution

The basic foundation of our democracy is the First Amendment guarantee of freedom of expression. The Opposing Viewpoints Series is dedicated to the concept of this basic freedom and the idea that it is more important to practice it than to enshrine it.

Interventions

Susan Hunnicutt, Book Editor

GREENHAVEN PRESS
A part of Gale, Cengage Learning

Detroit • New York • San Francisco • New Haven, Conn • Waterville, Maine • London

GALE
CENGAGE Learning·

Elizabeth Des Chenes, *Managing Editor*

© 2012 Greenhaven Press, a part of Gale, Cengage Learning

Gale and Greenhaven Press are registered trademarks used herein under license.

For more information, contact:
Greenhaven Press
27500 Drake Rd.
Farmington Hills, MI 48331-3535
Or you can visit our Internet site at gale.cengage.com.

For product information and technology assistance, contact us at:

Gale Customer Support, 1-800-877-4253.
For permission to use material from this text or product, submit all requests online at www.cengage.com/permissions.

Further permissions questions can be emailed to permissionrequest@cengage.com.

Articles in Greenhaven Press anthologies are often edited for length to meet page requirements. In addition, original titles of these works are changed to clearly present the main thesis and to explicitly indicate the author's opinion. Every effort is made to ensure the Greenhaven Press accurately reflects the original intent of the authors. Every effort has been made to trace the owners of copyrighted material.

Cover image © Ghislain & Marie David de Lossy/cultura/Corbis.

LIBRARY OF CONGRESS CATALOGING-IN-PUBLICATION DATA

Interventions / Susan Hunnicutt, book editor.
   p. cm. -- (Opposing viewpoints)
   Includes bibliographical references and index.
   ISBN 978-0-7377-6000-2 (hardcover) -- ISBN 978-0-7377-6001-9 (pbk.)
   1. Substance abuse. 2. Substance abuse--Treatment. 3. Substance abuse--Patients--Family relationships. 4. Substance abuse on television. I. Hunnicutt, Susan.
   HV4998.I588 2012
   616.86'06--dc23
                                                        2011037683

Printed in the United States of America
1 2 3 4 5 6 7 16 15 14 13 12

Contents

Chapter 1: Is Substance Abuse a Serious Problem?

Chapter 2: Is Intervention the Best Approach to Addiction?

Chapter 3: Who Should Be Involved in Substance Abuse Interventions?

Chapter 4: Should Interventions Be Televised?

Why Consider
Opposing Viewpoints?

"The only way in which a human being
can make some approach to knowing
the whole of a subject is by hearing
what can be said about it by persons of
every variety of opinion and studying
all modes in which it can be looked at
by every character of mind. No wise
man ever acquired his wisdom in any
mode but this."
                                    John Stuart Mill

In our media-intensive culture it is not difficult to find differing opinions. Thousands of newspapers and magazines and dozens of radio and television talk shows resound with differing points of view. The difficulty lies in deciding which opinion to agree with and which "experts" seem the most credible. The more inundated we become with differing opinions and claims, the more essential it is to hone critical reading and thinking skills to evaluate these ideas. Opposing Viewpoints books address this problem directly by presenting stimulating debates that can be used to enhance and teach these skills. The varied opinions contained in each book examine many different aspects of a single issue. While examining these conveniently edited opposing views, readers can develop critical thinking skills such as the ability to compare and contrast authors' credibility, facts, argumentation styles, use of persuasive techniques, and other stylistic tools. In short, the Opposing Viewpoints Series is an ideal way to attain the higher-level thinking and reading skills so essential in a culture of diverse and contradictory opinions.

In addition to providing a tool for critical thinking, Opposing Viewpoints books challenge readers to question their own strongly held opinions and assumptions. Most people form their opinions on the basis of upbringing, peer pressure, and personal, cultural, or professional bias. By reading carefully balanced opposing views, readers must directly confront new ideas as well as the opinions of those with whom they disagree. This is not to argue simplistically that everyone who reads opposing views will—or should—change his or her opinion. Instead, the series enhances readers' understanding of their own views by encouraging confrontation with opposing ideas. Careful examination of others' views can lead to the readers' understanding of the logical inconsistencies in their own opinions, perspective on why they hold an opinion, and the consideration of the possibility that their opinion requires further evaluation.

Evaluating Other Opinions

To ensure that this type of examination occurs, Opposing Viewpoints books present all types of opinions. Prominent spokespeople on different sides of each issue as well as well-known professionals from many disciplines challenge the reader. An additional goal of the series is to provide a forum for other, less known, or even unpopular viewpoints. The opinion of an ordinary person who has had to make the decision to cut off life support from a terminally ill relative, for example, may be just as valuable and provide just as much insight as a medical ethicist's professional opinion. The editors have two additional purposes in including these less known views. One, the editors encourage readers to respect others' opinions—even when not enhanced by professional credibility. It is only by reading or listening to and objectively evaluating others' ideas that one can determine whether they are worthy of consideration. Two, the inclusion of such viewpoints encourages the important critical thinking skill of objectively evaluating an author's credentials and bias. This evaluation will illuminate an author's reasons for taking a particular stance on an issue and will aid in readers' evaluation of the author's ideas.

It is our hope that these books will give readers a deeper understanding of the issues debated and an appreciation of the complexity of even seemingly simple issues when good and honest people disagree. This awareness is particularly important in a democratic society such as ours in which people enter into public debate to determine the common good. Those with whom one disagrees should not be regarded as enemies but rather as people whose views deserve careful examination and may shed light on one's own.

Thomas Jefferson once said that "difference of opinion leads to inquiry, and inquiry to truth." Jefferson, a broadly educated man, argued that "if a nation expects to be ignorant and free . . . it expects what never was and never will be." As individuals and as a nation, it is imperative that we consider the opinions of others and examine them with skill and discernment. The Opposing Viewpoints Series is intended to help readers achieve this goal.

David L. Bender and Bruno Leone,
Founders

Introduction

"By confronting the loved one with the consequences of the addiction, an intervention might penetrate the person's denial and help him or her decide to seek treatment."

Harvard Health Publications, 2011

"Addiction is a treatable disease and recovery is possible." This is one of the key messages of *Intervention*, an A&E Network series that documents the experiences of individuals whose lives and relationships have been derailed by their dependence on alcohol or drugs.

Every episode of *Intervention* follows a similar pattern, with the subjects introducing themselves, admitting that they have a problem, and describing how their addiction impacts a typical day. Personal storytelling is supported by film footage of the individual acquiring and using alcohol or drugs. These shots zoom in on lives in danger and disarray: unwashed dishes and unkempt hair; desperate forays out into the world to find drugs or alcohol; a woman cooking crack in her bed; nausea and disorientation; needles puncturing skin that is already bruised and broken; empty bottles and empty glasses and faces that are, alternately, anxious or stoned. Images of addiction are interpreted by the testimony of family members and close friends, who share the belief that the situation is at a crisis point, the subject's life is in danger, and something must be done.

Intervention moves on, in each episode, to detail the extent of personal tragedy, and the cost of addiction, in the life of the individual. Photos of happier times, before the subject became addicted, are an important part of the series' narrative, because they call attention to the beauty and the promise that has been or is being destroyed by substance abuse. Often, it is a parent who provides the narration. Each episode concludes with a staged intervention in which family members and friends are coached by one of the series' four interventionists: Jeff VanVonderen, Candy Finnigan, Rod Espudo, and John Southworth. Painstakingly constructed and emotional letters are read to the show's addict/subject. The letters convey love and concern, as well as feelings of hurt, anger, and loss, and they end in an ultimatum: either the addicted individual enters into treatment, or family members and friends will withdraw from the relationship.

Treatment, if it is accepted, takes place at a facility that has been carefully selected based on the individual's needs. It lasts for ninety days, with costs absorbed by the treatment center in return for being prominently featured in the final minutes of the show. The successful completion of a substance abuse rehabilitation program, which is the typical though not the inevitable ending to an episode of *Intervention*, holds out a message of hope that recovery from drug and alcohol abuse is possible not only for the individual whose story has just been shared, but for others as well.

As a series, *Intervention* plots the narrative of each show using a set of instructions developed in the 1960s by Vernon E. Johnson, an Episcopal priest who was himself in recovery, to help family members and friends break through an alcoholic's or addict's denial as well as their own enabling behaviors, in order to persuade their loved one to go into treatment. In May 2011 it was reported on the show's website that of 194 interventions presented since its initial episode in March of 2005, 151 individuals were still in recovery. The show won an Emmy in 2009 for Outstanding Reality Series, and it is also a five-time winner of the Entertainment Industries Council's Prism Award, which recognizes the accurate depiction of substance abuse and mental illness in film, television, and other forms of entertainment media.

While it is clear that *Intervention* makes good television, the show's portrayal of addiction and treatment has recently attracted criticism. In a 2011 article in the journal *Substance Use and Misuse*, Jason R. Kosovski and Douglas C. Smith, both of the University of Illinois at Champaign-Urbana, claim that inaccuracies in the show's storyline "perpetuate common myths about the definition and causes of addiction, what individuals can realistically expect from substance abuse treatment centers, and the typical outcomes of . . . treatments."

Kosovski and Smith's first criticism concerns a common technique of the reality genre that is employed by the producers of *Intervention*. The use of handheld cameras produces a "documentary gaze" and the impression of authenticity, spontaneity, objectivity, and authority. The show records unrehearsed scenes from the lives of the addicts whose stories it presents, which have included physical assaults on family members, intense emotional exchanges, and, frequently, illegal behavior. Such scenes, however, can be shot over weeks and even months and are heavily edited to fit into a one-hour time slot. Key scenes can be repeated multiple times. The result, according to Kosovski and Smith, is that "what appears on screen as real, spontaneous, and unscripted reality is actually the product of careful maneuvering by the show's producers."

Kosovski and Smith argue that reality television has a history of misrepresenting its subject matter, rooted in the stories it chooses to tell. In the case of *Intervention*, they say, the show stresses the role of childhood trauma and family dysfunction as the cause of addictive behaviors. This is a message that is repeated over and over, but that may not reflect the entire truth about why addiction occurs. "We are perfectly willing to believe . . . that addicts are often part of particular risk groups which can include those from broken homes and traumatized children and young adults. What *Intervention* does, however, is to depict their presence within these risk groups not as possible influences on addiction but rather as the sole and universal causes of such behaviors. In only rare exceptions do addicts featured on *Intervention* not belong to one or both of these groups." The show's emphasis on family dysfunction may result in a failure to explore other possible causes of addiction.

Another area where *Intervention* fails to accurately portray the culture of substance abuse, according to Kosovski and Smith, is in its presentation of the treatment experience. In the United States, substance abuse treatment in the public sector occurs almost wholly on an outpatient basis. Only 4 percent of treatment programs nationwide are private, for profit, inpatient enterprises like the ones that are featured on *Intervention*. The costs of private inpatient programs are quite high—often several thousand dollars per treatment episode—and typically are not covered or are only partially covered by many managed care insurance policies. Thus, the show holds out as ideal a form of treatment that is not accessible for most people.

Kosovski and Smith are also concerned that the show claims a very high rate of success both in persuading families to stage an intervention, and in persuading individuals to enter treatment following an intervention; this may create unrealistic expectations. They cite one study showing that as few as 30 percent of families that are encouraged to hold an intervention follow through and complete the process. "It is unclear why such a high percentage of the families on the show . . . complete their interventions, but this clearly does not represent what likely happens in real world community practice settings." They also note that few well-designed research studies have evaluated the outcomes of Johnson-style interventions, and that what research is available shows that a much smaller percentage of addicts actually enter treatment at the completion of an intervention.

The messages of the television series *Intervention*—that addiction is a treatable disease, that recovery is possible, and that those closest to an addicted person are in a position to have a significant impact on the course of the disease—are unquestionably valuable ones for individuals whose lives have been impacted by alcoholism and drug abuse. *Opposing Viewpoints: Interventions* addresses these and other topics in the following chapters: Is Substance Abuse a Serious Problem? Is Intervention the Best Approach to Addiction? Who Should Be Involved in Substance Abuse Interventions? Should Interventions Be Televised? Within this framework, the authors debate the controversies, issues, and media portrayal of interventions.

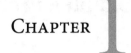

Chapter 1

Is Substance Abuse a Serious Problem?

Chapter Preface

In May 2011, the US Drug Enforcement Administration (DEA) sponsored its second National Prescription Drug Take-Back event, collecting more than 188 tons of unwanted or expired medications at 5,361 designated disposal sites around the country. Take-Back Day, which was aimed at removing excess supplies of controlled substances from home medicine cabinets, was planned in response to what some believe is an epidemic of prescription drug abuse. A survey conducted in 2009 by the Substance Abuse and Mental Health Services Administration (SAMHSA) found that 7 million Americans reported using a prescription medication for nonmedical purposes in the previous thirty days. Take-Back events make sense because more than 70 percent of those admitting to nonmedical use of prescription painkillers get them from friends or relatives, accessing unused home medicine cabinet supplies. "DEA is hard at work establishing a drug disposal process and will continue to offer take-back opportunities until the proper regulations are in place," explained Michele M. Leonhard, a DEA administrator involved in planning the Prescription Drug Take-Back. "With the support and hard work of our local law enforcement and community partners, these events have not only dramatically reduced the risk of prescription drug diversion and abuse, but have also increased awareness of this critical public health issue," she added.

The increase in the abuse of prescription medications is in part the result of changes in pain management strategies among health care professionals in recent decades. In the 1980s, opium-based painkillers were typically prescribed for cancer pain at the end of life. They were viewed as unsuitable for conditions such as arthritis, migraine, and back pain, because the dangers of tolerance, dependence, and addiction were too great. Pharmaceutical companies, hoping to expand the list of approved uses for these drugs, began combining opioids with other substances such as acetaminophen. They also created time-release products such as Oxycontin. Clinical trials were conducted to demonstrate the usefulness of these drugs for treatment of noncancer conditions, and case studies were published showing that addiction was unlikely to occur in patients who did not have a history of substance abuse, but who were suffering from chronic pain. The result is that between 1997 and 2007, the milligram-per-person use of prescription opioids increased more than 400 percent. In 2000, retail pharmacies dispensed 174 million prescriptions for opioids, but this number grew to 257 million prescriptions by 2009. Opiate overdoses, which were once almost always the result of heroin use, increasingly occur as a result of abuse of prescription painkillers.

It is commonly believed, according to a report released by the White House in 2011, that prescription drugs are less dangerous when abused than illegal drugs because they are approved by the Food and Drug Administration. "Many well-meaning parents do not understand the risks associated with giving prescribed medication to a teenager or another family member for whom the medication was not prescribed," the report noted. "Many parents are also not aware that youth are abusing prescription drugs; thus, they frequently leave unused prescription drugs in open medicine cabinets while making sure to lock their liquor cabinets."

Lack of awareness is, indeed, a key factor to consider in assessing the societal impact of substance abuse. Who is vulnerable, and what drugs are they using? Where does substance abuse occur? Should addiction be considered a behavioral problem, or is it a disease? These are some of the issues that are debated in the following chapter.

| "*The number of aging boomer addicts . . . continues to grow.*"

Addiction Rates Are Increasing Among Baby Boomers

Elaine Appleton Grant

Elaine Appleton Grant is a health reporter at New Hampshire Public Radio, where in 2010 she produced the series Prescription Drug Abuse in New Hampshire. *In this viewpoint she presents several examples of baby boomers whose families have staged interventions to get them into treatment, and who have subsequently been successful at overcoming their addictions to drugs and alcohol.*

As you read, consider the following questions:

1. How is intervention defined in this viewpoint?
2. According to the author, the stigma attached to addiction is easing and that is good news. Why?
3. While alcohol is the most commonly abused substance among older people, Grant mentions several drugs that are frequently connected with addiction among seniors. What are they?

In the predawn darkness of December 5, 2005, Patricia Dash woke her husband, Ron, and led him downstairs to the den of their house in New York. Ron was groggy—and confused, because standing by the fireplace was a stranger wearing a white turtleneck under a black sweater.

"What's a priest doing here?" he thought. "What the hell is going on?"

Maybe Ron was dreaming. Or maybe he'd drunk too much wine and vodka last night, or maybe it was the OxyContin and the Ambien he had popped along with the alcohol.

But the guy in the turtleneck wasn't alone. Perched nervously on the edge of the sofa were Ron's 8-year-old son, Sam; Ron's two older brothers; his 13-year-old niece; and his 86-year-old mother.

"Ron, say hello to Bob," said Patricia. "He's going to have a chat with you."

And that's when Ron got it: This was an intervention.

"She's gone way too far," thought Ron. Not only had Patricia recruited other family members for the intervention, but she had involved young Sammy.

A Loving but Direct Call to Arms

In the world of substance-abuse treatment, an intervention is a loving but direct call to arms, and often the last attempt by loved ones to end the destructive path of addiction. Patricia had hired Bob, an interventionist, to ensure that the family's initiative would succeed—and that no one would get hurt.

Ron scanned the faces in the room. He looked awful that morning—"like someone had hit him with a baseball bat," recalls Patricia. "He had gained a lot of weight and was all swollen." And he looked far older than his 52 years.

It hadn't always been this way. When Ron was enticed out of bachelorhood at 40 by his stunning Venezuelan bride, they had made an attractive and charismatic couple. They had also built a beautiful home: three stories with a bay view, an emblem of Ron's business success. Only a few years into their marriage, however, Ron began drinking at every possible occasion and started doing drugs more and more often. He became unpredictable, sullen, and sometimes violent.

Everyone Had a Chance to Speak

So this morning his family had no idea how Ron would react to their collective action to end the chaos. They had all written him letters explaining how much they loved him and how much they wanted—*needed*—him to get sober. Haltingly, each family member read him their letter. Sam had written that he'd lost his father and wanted him back.

"I was enraged," says Ron. He ran upstairs and grabbed the kitchen phone. "I was calling the cops to have everybody thrown out." Patricia, a slight size 4, threw herself at her bear of a husband. Ron shoved back. "If you don't go to rehab," Patricia screamed, "you'll never see me or Sammy again!"

And then Sam snapped.

"He marched to his bedroom and ripped up his letter," Ron says. "He grabbed a pen and carved the words 'I DON'T HAVE A DAD' in the doors of his closet. Then he came to me holding a picture of the two of us and cut it in half."

Seeing his little boy fall apart finally got through to Ron. "I saw—outside of myself—what I was doing to my loved ones. It broke me."

Ron fell down on his knees and grabbed for Sammy.

"Okay, I'm going," he said in tears. "I'm going."

Within hours, the family and Bob boarded a plane to Florida, where Ron was scheduled to enter residential treatment—*that day*—for alcoholism and drug addiction. At the Hanley Center in West Palm Beach, Ron would spend the next 48 hours in a sweaty, hazy, queasy detox, coming down from booze, tranquilizers, the narcotic painkiller OxyContin, and the sleeping medication Ambien. Only after the drugs had left his bloodstream would he begin the intense individual and group therapy, with about 30 other men from their 20s through their 50s, that would launch his life as a sober person.

A Growing Number of Aging Addicts

At 57, Ron has been sober and straight for more than five years. The number of aging boomer addicts, however, continues to grow. The result: the first sizable population of over-50 adults to struggle not just with alcohol but also with drugs, according to the Substance Abuse and Mental Health Services Administration (SAMHSA), a federal agency. And as the nation's 77 million baby boomers age, the agency predicts, the number of drug addicts who qualify for senior discounts will only grow. In a report published in December 2009, SAMHSA disclosed that 4.3 million adults age 50 and older had used an illicit drug in the preceding year. The number of boomers with substance-abuse problems will double from 2.5 million in 1999 to 5 million in 2020, the agency forecasts. Not surprisingly, SAMHSA projects that the need for treatment will also double, as longtime abusers gain greater access to prescription meds.

The explosion in midlife drug abuse is tearing families apart, ruining careers, destroying addicts' health, and driving up health care costs. But not *all* the news is bad: The social stigma of addiction, though still present, is easing as it becomes clear that addicts are neighbors, friends, grandmothers, husbands. That awareness forces fewer addicts underground. Plus, it makes them more willing to seek help than yesterday's alcoholics were. Rehab is no magic solution, but when older addicts find the right treatment—be it a local 12-step meeting or an inpatient rehab program—recovery can transform a family's life.

In 2005—the same year that Ron Dash checked into the Hanley Center—Fred Blow, Ph.D., noticed "a lot more boomers suddenly coming into treatment programs with cocaine problems." Says Blow, a leading researcher on aging and addiction: "We'd never seen that before in this population." This new crop of coke users, he says, are middle-aged, middle-class, and often retired. And now their free time is killing them: When retirement is bereft of fulfilling activities, Blow says, some people turn to drugs to fill the void.

Blow, professor of psychiatry at the University of Michigan Medical School, recalls a 58-year-old retiree who had taught school for 30 years. "He had smoked a little marijuana before," says Blow, "but never had a problem. Now here he is entering treatment for a full-blown addiction to crack cocaine. He had too much time on his hands and turned to coke to cope." One-third of boomers who enter treatment qualify as these "late-onset" addicts, Blow estimates. "This trend is going to continue," he says. "We need to be prepared for it."

Multiple Addictions Common

Though alcohol remains the most commonly abused substance among the upper age brackets, drug use is rising. Among those age 50 and up, treatment-facility admissions for cocaine abuse quadrupled from 1992 to 2008; for heroin abuse they more than doubled. Prescription-medication and marijuana abuse also climbed significantly. "Whereas alcohol was the dominant, singular problem pushing people into treatment in the past," Blow says, "now we're seeing more cases of a multiple-substance-abuse problem—people using alcohol plus marijuana, or alcohol plus cocaine."

The easy availability of addictive prescription drugs magnifies this lethal mix. Over the past 20 years many doctors have become more aggressive in treating pain, making opium-based (and synthetic opioid) painkillers some of the most widely prescribed drugs in the United States. In 2009 alone, doctors wrote 128 million prescriptions for hydrocodone-acetaminophen combination products such as Vicodin.

These powerful painkillers spare legitimate patients a lot of agony. But many of these drugs also cause euphoria. And that makes them highly addictive. . . .

Addiction Less Recognized in Elders

According to the National Institute on Alcohol Abuse and Alcoholism, while hospital admissions for alcohol-related problems are equal to those for heart attacks among older Americans, physicians and nurses are "significantly less likely to recognize alcoholism in an older patient than in a younger patient."

The Partnership at Drugfree.org, July 20, 2003. www.drugfree.org.

Elders Metabolize Drugs Differently

Steve Bartels, M.D., director of the Dartmouth Centers for Health and Aging in Lebanon, New Hampshire, warns his patients about the body's declining ability to metabolize drugs as they age. "Older adults who may be abusing marijuana, cocaine, or other drugs are sensitive to smaller amounts than when they were younger," he says. "The problem is, they don't know that. So they get into trouble—motor vehicle accidents, domestic incidents—at much lower levels of use."

Substance abuse in an older adult mimics many of the signs of aging: It causes memory loss, cognitive problems, tremors, and falls. The upshot is that even family members may not be able to recognize that a loved one is an addict. Late-stage abuse—especially in women only 55 or 60 years old—induces weight loss, muscle wasting, and, among alcoholics, elevated rates of breast cancer. "Addiction will move you into 'old old' very quickly," says interventionist Debra Jay, coauthor of *Aging and Addiction*. "You may be healthy, a runner, a vegan—but if you're doing cocaine or any other drug or alcohol, your body will break down much faster at 55 than it will at 35." The rise in boomer drug use is perhaps unsurprising. This is the generation, after all, that made drug experimentation mainstream, so today's 55-year-old addict is often yesterday's high school stoner. At least two-thirds of boomers who wind up in treatment have been drinking, taking drugs, or doing both for the bulk of their adult lives—and during some of their teen years, as well. "The earlier your onset, the worse your problem," says John Dyben, the Hanley Center's clinical director.

Ron Dash first smoked pot at 13 and "loved it from the start," he says. "I grew up reading about [Beat Generation poet] Allen Ginsberg and [LSD-advocating psychiatrist] Timothy Leary. For a kid like me, who wanted to be different, to get attention, pot was cool." And for him it led to hash, cocaine, mushrooms, and LSD, often amplified by alcohol.

Dyben also points to the boomer proclivity to medicate both physical and emotional pain. "So here I am as a baby boomer, hitting 50," Dyben says, role-playing the midlife everyman. "My knees hurt a little more when I play tennis, and from the culture I grew up in I have the mind-set that says, 'If I'm hurting, something's wrong. And if something's wrong, a pill will fix it.' But the idea of better living through chemistry'—that you can feel better by taking a pill, or by smoking or drinking something—that mind-set is killing boomers."

Doctors Arm Patients with Pills

Many doctors unwittingly collude with addicts to keep them armed with pills. Russ C., a 61-year-old retired tree-worker supervisor and a grandfather, began taking narcotic pain relievers after a work-related neck injury at 37. Over the years he took more and more narcotics and tranquilizers to tamp down the pain. By 2003 he was in such agony he had to leave his job. He went on disability and experienced a severe depression—a not-uncommon consequence of job loss or retirement. "All I had to do was sit around and take pills," he says. By 2005 "it got to where my wife was afraid to come home from work. Would she find me dead on the floor?"

At age 56, desperate to kick his habit, Russ turned to a psychiatrist—who gave him a bit of misguided advice that outrages him to this day. "You're much too old, and you've been on pain meds far too long, to detox," the doctor told him. Instead he prescribed methadone, piling it atop the other medications he knew Russ was taking. "He told me to make myself as comfortable as possible for however long my life would be," says Russ.

On methadone, he says, "I had no feelings. I thought God had taken my soul and my heart. I couldn't drive. My memory was gone." He was so unstable that his grown children refused to leave him alone with his grandchildren. Says Russ: "I had no purpose to my life."

It was just as bad, if not worse, for his wife, Kathy, now 59. She met Russ while she was still in high school; they married the day after she graduated from junior college. Almost 40 years on, she is still devoted to him. But his illness was eating her life whole. "On methadone he constantly wanted coffee so he wouldn't become comatose," she says. "But as fast as you could snap your fingers, he would nod off and spill scalding coffee all over himself. Things like that would happen five or six times a day."

Kathy paid dearly for her husband's addiction: "I couldn't devote my attention to the grandchildren because I had to take care of Russ," she says. "It wasn't just one person who had this disease. We were *all* disabled by it."

By 2007 Russ had dropped from 170 to 118 pounds. Terrified by her husband's deterioration, Kathy and their kids began looking for a rehab facility. But they said nothing to Russ. "We felt seeking treatment had to be his choice," Kathy recalls.

Looking for a Safe Place

Finally Russ felt he could no longer function. He had to quit the painkillers. But he dreaded repeating an experience from two years earlier, when he spent seven rough days at an inner-city detox center. "People drove through the parking lot at night, shouting through the windows at patients," says Kathy. "They had lockdowns; they had body searches. We didn't know every rehab's not like that."

Loath to endure another such experience, Russ resolved to quit methadone on his own. "I had violent shakes," he recalls. "I was vomiting. I could feel my organs trembling in my body." Kathy, conceding she couldn't help him by herself, reached her limit on November 12, 2007. "We've found a place that would be good for you," she told Russ. "Will you go?"

Russ agreed, and Kathy promptly called their kids. Together they drove Russ from his home in southern California to Community Bridges in Mesa, Arizona. Russ doubted he would survive the nine-hour trip. "I didn't want to die in front of my family," he says.

He spent 10 days in detox, then transferred to Journey Healing Centers in Scottsdale for 45 days of rehab. This time, the treatment worked. (Patients are far less likely to relapse if—as Russ was—they're surrounded by a supportive, sober family.)

Russ has been clean for three years. Though he doesn't talk about it, Kathy says he's in pain every day but simply tolerates it. What he *does* talk about is the thrill of rejoining his family. He plays often with his eight grandkids and even babysits them. "Not a night goes by," he says, "that I don't thank God for this second chance." . . .

Some Things Have Changed

In prior generations the shame associated with addiction often kept people from seeking treatment. But midlife addicts— and, crucially, their spouses—are far more open to confronting thorny issues. "Younger spouses aren't willing to take secrets to their graves," says interventionist Debra Jay.

That makes boomers likelier than their parents to seek therapy. Yet even patients who can afford it must hunt hard for rehab of any kind. Treatment programs across the country have dwindled in the past two decades. Says Fred Blow: "That's something we're going to have to face as a nation; we must have more treatment programs. Older people can advocate for that."

Five years after the intervention that changed his life, Ron Dash remains clean and sober. Patricia, Ron, and Sam now live in Florida, where Ron bikes, swims, and attends 12-step meetings in between driving Sam to football practice and cooking dinner. "After being pretty much absent all those years, Ron has learned to be Sam's father," says Patricia. "And he has learned to be his friend."

Despite the odds against them, she and Ron have rebuilt their marriage. It didn't happen the day he walked out of rehab, nor in the weeks and months afterward. "I spent four years waiting for the other shoe to drop," Patricia admits. "Not until this year have I finally started trusting him again."

"That was huge," says Ron, pondering how his life might be otherwise. "What happens to Sammy if we go through all this trouble and the addict, the alcoholic, doesn't stay sober?"

He plans never to find out.

VIEWPOINT *2*

> *"Full-time students [who] meet the medical criteria for substance abuse and dependence . . . is two and one half times more than [that of] the general population."*

Substance Abuse Is a Problem on College Campuses

UniversityChic.com

The author in the following viewpoint outlines the results of a study carried out by the National Center on Addiction and Substance Abuse (CASA) at Columbia University. The study shows that increasing numbers of college students are abusing drugs and alcohol, and argues that college administrators are not doing enough to combat the problem. UniversityChic.com is a cultural website geared to college women.

As you read, consider the following questions:

1. How many college students abuse drugs and alcohol, according to CASA's report, *Wasting the Best and the Brightest*, as cited by the author?
2. What happened to the rate of drug and alcohol abuse on college campuses between 1993 and 2005, according to UniversityChic.com?

3. The author says drug use has become a what on college
   and university campuses?

The college experience does not begin and end with the classroom. Part of the college experience is socializing, participating in campus activities, joining a sorority or fraternity, as well as partying. But according to the National Center on Addiction and Substance Abuse at Columbia University (CASA), the partying atmosphere at college campuses may be getting out of control. The organization released a 231-page report [in 2007] detailing the rise in drinking and drug abuse at college campuses nationwide.

The report, titled *Wasting the Best and the Brightest: Substance Abuse at America's Colleges and Universities*, stated that 3.8 million full-time college students binge drink and/or abuse prescription and illegal drugs. The report also cited that 1.8 million full-time students meet the medical criteria for substance abuse and dependence, which is two and one half times more than the general population who meet the same criteria. In the CASA's press release for *Wasting the Best and the Brightest*, Joseph A. Califano, president and chairman for the CASA, said, "It's time to take the 'high' out of higher education. Under any circumstances acceptance by administrators, trustees, professors, and parents of this college culture of alcohol and drug abuse is inexcusable."

More Students Are Using

The CASA's report is a compilation of over four years of research and other methodology. The press release states that this report is the "most extensive examination ever undertaken" regarding the problem of substance abuse that occurs on college campuses within the United States. Although findings showed that from 1993 to 2005 there was no decline in the proportion of students who drink, the increase occurred in the intensity of excessive drinking and drug abuse. The report found that between the years of 1993 and 2005:

- The proportion of students who binge drink rose 16 percent, students who get drunk at least three times a month rose 25 percent, and students who drink to get drunk rose 21 percent.
- The proportion of students that abuse prescription drugs also rose with the highest percentage increase shown in the use of tranquilizers such as Xanax and Valium.
- The proportion of students that abuse illegal drugs, marijuana excluded, rose 52 percent. The daily use of marijuana doubled.

Another relevant finding from the report stated members of fraternities and sororities have higher percentage rates of binge drinking, drinking, drinking and driving while intoxicated, and using illegal substances than non-members. Thirty-seven percent of college students are prevented from seeking help because of fear that a social stigma will be attached. There was also a higher percentage of sexual intercourse between students who use illegal drugs than those who do not.

A Rite of Passage

The CASA reports that the problem stems from the idea that using drugs while in college is a rite of passage, which makes it difficult for college administrators to overcome this perception and combat the issue. Califano says that "by failing to become part of the solution, these Pontius Pilate presidents and parents, deans, trustees, and alumni have become part of the problem. Their acceptance of the status quo of rampant alcohol and other drug abuse puts the best and the brightest and the nation's future in harm's way." The CASA however does propose to try to offer a solution, 10 as a matter of fact. The CASA's website, www.casacolumbia.org, cites 10 key actions that will assist in the prevention and reduction of the substance abuse issue facing the nation's colleges:

- Set clear substance use policies and consequences of violations.

College Student Past Year Drug Use, 1993–2005 (percent)

	1993	2005
Any illicit drug	30.6	36.6
Marijuana	27.9	33.3
Hallucinogens	6.0	5.0
Inhalants	3.8	1.8
Cocaine	2.7	5.7
Ecstasy	0.8	2.9
Heroin	0.1	0.3

Based on data from L.D. Johnston, P.M. O'Malley, J.G. Bachman, and J.E. Schulenberg, *Monitoring the Future: National Results on Adolescent Drug Use: Overview of Key Findings, 2005*, Bethesda MD: National Institute on Drug Abuse, 2006.

TAKEN FROM: *Wasting the Best and the Brightest: Substance Abuse at America's Colleges and Universities*, National Center on Addiction and Substance Abuse at Columbia University, March 2007.

• Ban smoking; prohibit alcohol and tobacco ads, sponsorships and promotions on campus; ban alcohol in dorms, in most common areas, at on-campus student parties and at college sporting events.

• Screen all students for substance abuse problems; target high-risk students and times; provide needed interventions and treatment.

• Hold student classes and exams Monday through Friday to reduce weekend substance abuse.

• Educate faculty, staff, students, parents and alumni about substance abuse and involve them in prevention activities.

• Engage students in service learning courses and community service.

- Offer substance-free recreational opportunities.
- Include in the academic curricula information about substance abuse and addiction.
- Engage community partners in prevention, enforcement, interventions and treatment.
- Monitor rates and consequences of student substance use and evaluate and improve programs and services.

Changes Are Needed

Since the release of the report, there has been no national response from colleges offering solutions to combat the issue. Steps to thwart this problem are being done by the colleges individually.

College itself is a rite of passage. It is the passing from a teenager into young adulthood while developing the skills that he/she will take with them as they go off into world to find the path that ultimately leads to their destiny. Because the use of alcohol and drugs has been considered a customary part of the college experience, it may be difficult for parents, alumni, and professors to develop a "do as I say not as I did" approach.

However, if the excessive use of drinking and drugs is beginning to overshadow the entire college experience, then maybe it is time parents, alumni, and college faculty begin to take the steps to change the perception of what the college experience really is.

*"According to labor statistics, vast
majorities of the people who are drug
users, heavy or binge drinkers or have
other substance abuse problems, are
employed."*

Substance Abuse Is a Problem in the Workplace

James Schuster, as told to Smart Business Network

*James Schuster is the chief medical officer at Community Care,
a behavioral health organization that is part of the University of
Pittsburgh Medical Center. In this viewpoint, from an interview
of Schuster with the Smart Business Network, Schuster argues that
addiction is a serious workplace issue that can lead to increased
absenteeism and reduced productivity. He discusses signs of addiction and options for addressing a substance abuse problem that is
interfering with an employee's performance.*

As you read, consider the following questions:

1. According to Schuster, how common is it for individuals
   with substance abuse issues to be employed?
2. What are some of the ways that substance abuse can impact the workplace, as told by Schuster?

3. What are employee assistance programs and what role do they play in addressing addiction in the workplace, according to the author?

Substance abuse and addiction are serious problems throughout society, so it only makes sense that the problem carries over into the workplace. According to labor statistics, vast majorities of the people who are drug users, heavy or binge drinkers or have other substance abuse problems, are employed.

A 2007 survey indicated that 8.4 percent of all full-time workers used illicit drugs and 8.8 percent reported heavy alcohol use. "There is a cost to addiction that impacts the workplace and should be of concern to all employers," says James Schuster, MD, MBA, the chief medical officer for Community Care, a behavioral health organization that is part of the UPMC [University of Pittsburgh Medical Center] Insurance Services Division. "The cost in terms of productivity can often be substantial."

Smart Business spoke with Schuster about addiction in the workplace and what employers need to know about it.

Smart Business: How does addiction or substance abuse manifest itself in the workplace?

James Schuster: The most obvious effects are absenteeism, reduced productivity and tension between the employer and the employee. You can also see its effects in increased accidents and decreased productivity. Because addiction impacts every facet of a person's life, the problem needs to be addressed at many different levels, including in the workplace. Dependency on drugs or alcohol can severely compromise an employee's ability to contribute to the success of the company.

In addition, addiction does not just impact the employee. Nearly 40 percent of industrial fatalities and 47 percent of industrial injuries can be tied to alcohol consumption or alcoholism. The U.S. Department of Labor estimates that employees who

Impaired on the Job

The vast majority of drug users are employed, and when they arrive for work, they don't leave their problems at the door. Of the 17.2 million illicit drug users aged 18 or older in 2005, 12.9 million (74.8 percent) were employed either full or part time. Furthermore, research indicates that between 10 and 20 percent of the nation's workers who die on the job test positive for alcohol or other drugs. In fact, industries with the highest rates of drug use are the same as those at a high risk for occupational injuries, such as construction, mining, manufacturing and wholesale.

US Department of Labor, Occupational Safety and Health Administration, July 2, 2007. www.osha.gov.

abuse substances are 25 to 30 percent less productive and miss work three times more often than non-abusing employees.

How can an employer know if an employee has an addiction issue?

This is not always easy and that fact only compounds the problem. There are few explicit warning signs connected to it. Also, many addicts are almost experts in hiding their addiction from others.

Diagnosing a substance abuse problem is not something an employer should ever do, but there are signs to look for that may indicate that an employee may be a substance abuser. Extreme fluctuations in mood and productivity, for instance, can be indicative. Alcoholism is often connected with slurred speech, belligerent behavior and decreased inhibition. Frequent tardiness, unexplained absences and unusual weight loss or gain can also be signs.

What should employers do if they suspect an employee of alcohol or drug abuse?

As an employer, you should be focused on helping the employee get back on track, not offering a diagnosis for his or her condition. There is no need to form an opinion of your employee based on his or her addiction. It is important to understand that substance abuse definitely has the markers of a disease. There are clear genetic relationships and people who metabolize alcohol more quickly are more likely to have alcohol problems.

When should an employer do something about an employee's substance abuse?

If the employee's drug use directly affects his or her performance at work and relationships with co-workers, an employer can justify taking some kind of action. A logical first step would be to refer the employee to human resources, or, if possible, an Employee Assistance Program (EAP). An accurate assessment of the problem is possible by following this route and an EAP can assist with an evaluation of disciplinary options if needed.

Employers should also start by refusing to "enable" the employee. The employee needs to be held accountable for his or her actions. He should not be permitted to continue his self-destructive behavior at work. This limitation must be communicated to supervisors and co-workers alike.

Can the workplace be an effective place to deal with substance abuse?

Yes. For one thing, the workplace can serve as a framework to counteract the denial and manipulation that often goes with alcoholism. An employee needs to work to make money and the risk of losing that can be strong motivation to get help for problems. The workplace is also the best place where behavior patterns can be accurately documented and that documentation can convince an employee to seek help and change behavior.

EAPs were originally created to deal specifically with alcohol problems, so it is not surprising that studies have shown that 70 to 80 percent of persons with alcoholism who are referred to EAP programs are productive employees within one year after being referred to a program.

Are small businesses affected by addiction and substance abuse?

Yes, they are. In fact, smaller businesses might be more adversely affected. Roughly half of all U.S. workers are employed by a small business—that is, a company with 500 or fewer workers—and 90 percent of small businesses employ either current illicit drug users or heavy drinkers. However, smaller firms are generally less likely to test for substance abuse and less likely to offer programs designed to combat the problem.

Can addiction problems be completely handled in the workplace?

That would be extremely rare. It is difficult to overcome an addiction without some kind of outside help. An employee needs the encouragement and support of his or her employer to make it through, but that person may need more than the workplace can provide.

| "We now know that the implementation
of workplace drug testing programs
has significantly reduced drug abuse
in worker populations subject to drug
testing."

Substance Abuse in the Workplace Is Declining

Marketwire

In this viewpoint Marketwire, a newswire service for online press release distribution, describes how tests used by employers to detect drug use also deter drug use. Marketwire asserts that testing shows a 19-year decline in workplace abuse of cocaine and methamphetamine.

As you read, consider the following questions:

1. This viewpoint discusses two reasons that employers often implement drug tests. What are they?
2. What are some reasons listed in the viewpoint that account for the decline of workplace drug abuse?
3. Do you think the author presents persuasive evidence that drug use is declining in the workplace?

Cocaine use among U.S. employees and job applicants in the general U.S. workforce declined sharply in 2008, according to the annual Quest Diagnostics Drug Testing Index (DTI), based on 5.7 million urine drug tests performed last year by Quest Diagnostics, the nation's leading provider of drug testing services. In addition, methamphetamine use in the general workforce declined year over year, yet positive urine tests for amphetamine showed an uptick in worker use of this stimulant drug.

"We now know that the implementation of workplace drug testing programs has significantly reduced drug abuse in worker populations subject to drug testing," according to Robert Willette, Ph.D., President of Duo Research and former Chief of the Research Technology Branch of the National Institute on Drug Abuse. "This impact is evidenced in a variety of surveys and other data sources, one of the most valuable being the Quest Diagnostics Drug Testing Index. While many substances are showing declines in use, a significant trend upward that will be important to watch is the rise in amphetamine positives. This coincides with survey and emergency room data, and could be tied to the significant increase in drugs prescribed for Attention Deficit/Hyperactivity Disorder (ADHD). Similar trends are seen with the increased use and abuse of pain medications."

Employers that implement drug testing programs do so for a variety of reasons, most often to protect the health and well-being of employees and avert business risk associated with drug-induced judgments. The 2008 DTI summarizes 7.3 million urine drug test results of the U.S. workforce, including both the general U.S. workforce and federally mandated safety-sensitive workforce, which includes pilots, bus drivers, and nuclear power plant operators. The DTI looks at "recent use," as measured by laboratory analysis of a urine sample, which detects drug use within the prior one to three days.

Overall recent drug use in the combined U.S. workforce has sustained a 19-year decline since Quest Diagnostics first published the Drug Testing Index in 1989, summarizing data from

1988, when 13.6 percent of workers tested positive for drug use. In 2008, 3.6 percent of the combined U.S. workforce tested positive in a urine drug test compared to 3.8 percent in 2007. Experts credit effective drug testing programs with positively influencing worker behavior and, in recent years, have cited law enforcement's impact on the decreased availability and increasing costs of illicit substances as a factor in recent drug use declines.

Cocaine and Methamphetamine Use Decline Sharply

Positivity rates of recent use of cocaine in the general U.S. workforce dropped 29 percent (0.58 percent of all urine drug tests in 2007 to 0.41 percent in 2008) continuing a steep decline. In 2006, 0.72 percent of urine tests showed recent use of cocaine. While methamphetamine positivity in the general U.S. workforce also dropped 21 percent (0.14 percent in 2007 to 0.11 percent in 2008), the positivity rate for amphetamine increased more than 12 percent, from 0.40 percent to 0.45 percent.

Cocaine, methamphetamine and amphetamine are each a type of stimulant, typically used to increase alertness and relieve fatigue. Stimulants are also used for euphoric effects or may be used to counteract the "down" feeling of tranquilizers or alcohol. Possible side effects of stimulants include increased heart and respiratory rates, elevated blood pressure, dilated pupils and decreased appetite. High doses may cause irregular heartbeat, loss of coordination or collapse. Indications of possible misuse may include excessive activity, talkativeness, irritability or nervousness.

Random Drug Testing Programs Deter Use

Random drug testing programs appear to deter drug use, DTI data show. In the federally mandated safety-sensitive workforce, where employees expect random drug testing, the drug positivity rate is far lower than the rate of positivity among job applicants in that same workforce. However, in the general workforce, where employees are far less likely to expect random drug testing, the drug use positivity rate is dramatically higher than that of job applicants.

"At first, it may not be surprising that in the safety-sensitive workforce random drug test positivity is nearly 18 percent lower than pre-employment positivity," according to Barry Sample, Ph.D., Director of Science and Technology for Quest Diagnostics' Employer Solutions Division. "Pre-employment drug testing is an important frontline filter to help ensure a drug-free workforce. However, we see a more complex story when these rates are compared to the general workforce, where employees are far less likely to expect random drug testing. Here, the random urine test positivity rate is 47 percent higher than the pre-employment urine test positivity rate."

Random urine test positivity among safety-sensitive workers was 1.4 percent, according to the 2008 DTI, nearly 18 percent lower than the pre-employment positivity rate of 1.7 percent. Those employed in the safety-sensitive workforce understand that they can be subject to a random drug test at any time. In the general workforce, where random urine testing is not typically required of employees nor expected, the random urine test positivity rate was 47 percent higher than that workforce's pre-employment positivity rate. The general U.S. workforce pre-employment urine testing positivity rate reached 3.6 percent, while the general U.S. workforce random urine testing positivity rate reached 5.3 percent.

| "*Addictions often create interpersonal problems for all family members.*"

Drug and Alcohol Abuse Damages Family Relationships

Beth Aileen Lameman

In this viewpoint Beth Aileen Lameman, a writer for Healthkey .com, argues that substance abuse damages family relationships. She considers family therapy as an option for those whose family lives are impacted by drug or alcohol abuse.

As you read, consider the following questions:

1. According to the author, what are some of the causes of family conflict caused by substance abuse?
2. What are some of the health problems Lameman mentions in connection with alcohol abuse?
3. Does the author think that family therapy can always be helpful for the families of substance abusers?

Drug and alcohol abuse not only affects the abuser and his/ her life, but also the lives of family members. When recovery begins, your whole family should be involved when possible.

Family therapy is a good option for recovery with substance abuse.

Problems for Families

Drug and alcohol abuse not only affects you, but also your family. Addictions often create interpersonal problems for all family members.

1. *Jealousy*: You can grow jealous of your friends, your partner, other family members and other people in your life. Your partner may also be jealous and resentful of you.

2. *Conflict with Partner*: You may have arguments, get/give the "silent treatment" or grow apart by putting your addiction first.

3. *Conflict with Children*: You may argue with your children and they may disregard your authority or be afraid of you.

4. *Conflict over Money*: You may struggle economically because of losing your job, taking time off from your job, making poor financial choices or simply pouring your money into your addiction.

5. *Emotional Trauma*: You may create emotional hardships for your partner and/or your children by yelling, talking down, insulting or manipulating.

6. *Violence*: You may become violent or your family members may become violent with you, including slapping, hitting or smashing or throwing objects.

7. *Cheating*: You may become distant from your partner and seek satisfaction through pornography, Internet sex, prostitution or someone else in your life who you feel "understands" you.

8. *Separation*: Your behavior due to addiction may cause separation, divorce, and/or isolation from other family members, particularly children, either because they've been taken from you or because they don't want to be around you.

9. *Patterns*: Your life example will influence your partner, your children and other family members. There is a high likelihood that your children will become addicted to drugs or alcohol.

10. *Health Risks*: Drinking while pregnant can cause fetal alcohol syndrome—damage to the baby's brain. Smoking in the household can cause health problems for family members from secondhand smoke, including lung cancer. Being under the influence of drugs and alcohol will overall impair your judgment and can lead to neglect or harm.

Family Structures Are Compromised

Drug and alcohol abuse affects different family structures in different ways. These family structures are adapted from The Substance Abuse and Mental Health Services "Substance Abuse Treatment and Family Therapy" guide:

- *You live alone or with a partner*: Both of you need help. If one of you has an addiction and the other doesn't, you'll suffer from issues of co-dependence.

- *You live with a spouse or partner and young children*: Parents' problems affect children. Often, one parent has an addiction and the other protects the children or assumes more parental responsibilities. If both parents have addictions, the effect on children is worse. Your addiction is likely to pass down to your children.

- *You have a step-family*: Substance abuse impedes your step-family's integration and stability.

- *You are older and have grown children*: Family resources are needed to treat an older adult's substance abuse. Elder maltreatment may become an issue.

- *You are younger and live with your family*: The needs and concerns of siblings or other family members may get ignored because of crises caused by substance abuse. If you

Chaotic and Unpredictable

In families where alcohol or other drugs are being abused, behavior is frequently unpredictable and communication is unclear. Family life is characterized by chaos and unpredictability. Behavior can range from loving to withdrawn to crazy. Structure and rules may be either nonexistent or inconsistent. Children, who may not understand that their parent's behavior and mood is determined by the amount of alcohol or other drugs in their bloodstream, can feel confused and insecure. They love their parents and worry about them, and yet feel angry and hurt that their parents do not love them enough to stop using.

Phoenix House's Center on Addiction and the Family. http://coaf.org.

also have a parent who has a substance abuse problem, you're in danger of physical and/or emotional conflicts.

Family Therapy May Help

According to the "Substance Abuse Treatment and Family Therapy" guide, family therapy is a good resource for recovery for family members with drug and alcohol addictions.

How can family therapy help me?

• Your family's strengths and resources can help you find ways to live without alcohol and drug addiction.

• You and your family will be better able to deal with the impact of detoxification, the process of cleansing your body from an addiction.

• Your family will become more aware of their own needs

and feel that they can express their needs safely.

• The next generation in your family will be less likely to carry on your addiction.

• If you have lost custody of your children, you will be better able to overcome your addiction and reconnect with your family.

What should I know about family therapy?

• Make sure you find the right therapist or counselor and that you're upfront about why your family is going to therapy. Family therapists often don't screen for substance abuse, while substance abuse counselors need proper training and licensing to practice family therapy.

• If there is any physical or emotional abuse in the family, family counseling techniques are not an option, because family members must be protected.

| *"Addiction is a chronic, often relapsing brain disease."*

Drug Addiction Is a Brain Disease

National Institute on Drug Abuse

The National Institute on Drug Abuse (NIDA), a member of the National Institutes of Health, supports research aimed at improving prevention and treatment of substance abuse and addiction. In the following viewpoint NIDA argues that addiction is a chronic and relapsing disease affecting the brain. Like other diseases, treatment can be effective and recovery is possible; however, it is not uncommon for relapses to occur, NIDA maintains.

As you read, consider the following questions:

1. According to the author, what are the estimated monetary costs associated with tobacco, alcohol, and other drugs?
2. How do drugs interfere with the brain's ability to send and receive information, according to NIDA?
3. What are some of the factors that determine whether a person will become addicted, as listed by the author?

DrugAbuse.gov, "NIDA InfoFacts: Understanding Drug Abuse and Addiction," February 2011. Copyright © 2011 by National Institute on Drug Abuse. All rights reserved. Reproduced by permission.

Many people do not understand why or how other people become addicted to drugs. It can be wrongfully assumed that drug abusers lack moral principles or willpower and that they could stop using drugs simply by choosing to change their behavior. In reality, drug addiction is a complex disease, and quitting takes more than good intentions. In fact, because drugs change the brain in ways that foster compulsive drug abuse, quitting is difficult, even for those who are ready to do so. Through scientific advances, we know more about how drugs work in the brain than ever, and we also know that drug addiction can be successfully treated to help people stop abusing drugs and lead productive lives.

Drug abuse and addiction have negative consequences for individuals and for society. Estimates of the total overall costs of substance abuse in the United States, including productivity and health- and crime-related costs, exceed $600 billion annually. This includes approximately $193 billion for illicit drugs, $193 billion for tobacco, and $235 billion for alcohol. As staggering as these numbers are, they do not fully describe the breadth of destructive public health and safety implications of drug abuse and addiction, such as family disintegration, loss of employment, failure in school, domestic violence, and child abuse.

What Is Drug Addiction?

Addiction is a chronic, often relapsing brain disease that causes compulsive drug seeking and use, despite harmful consequences to the addicted individual and to those around him or her. Although the initial decision to take drugs is voluntary for most people, the brain changes that occur over time challenge a person's self-control and ability to resist intense impulses urging them to take drugs.

Fortunately, treatments are available to help people counter addiction's powerful disruptive effects. Research shows that combining addiction treatment medications with behavioral therapy is the best way to ensure success for most patients. Treatment

Drug Abuse Changes the Brain

Research has revealed that addiction affects the brain circuits involved in reward, motivation, memory, and inhibitory control. When these circuits are disrupted, so is a person's capacity to freely choose not to use drugs, even when it means losing everything they used to value. In fact, the inability to stop is the essence of addiction, like riding in a car with no brakes.

National Institute on Drug Abuse,
Addiction Science: From Molecules to
Managed Care. *www.nida.nih.gov.*

approaches that are tailored to each patient's drug abuse patterns and any co-occurring medical, psychiatric, and social problems can lead to sustained recovery and a life without drug abuse.

Similar to other chronic, relapsing diseases, such as diabetes, asthma, or heart disease, drug addiction can be managed successfully. And as with other chronic diseases, it is not uncommon for a person to relapse and begin abusing drugs again. Relapse, however, does not signal treatment failure—rather, it indicates that treatment should be reinstated, adjusted, or that an alternative treatment is needed to help the individual regain control and recover.

Your Brain on Drugs

Drugs contain chemicals that tap into the brain's communication system and disrupt the way nerve cells normally send, receive, and process information. There are at least two ways that drugs cause this disruption: (1) by imitating the brain's natural chemical messengers and (2) by overstimulating the "reward circuit" of the brain.

53

Some drugs (e.g., marijuana and heroin) have a similar structure to chemical messengers called neurotransmitters, which are naturally produced by the brain. This similarity allows the drugs to "fool" the brain's receptors and activate nerve cells to send abnormal messages.

Other drugs, such as cocaine or methamphetamine, can cause the nerve cells to release abnormally large amounts of natural neurotransmitters (mainly dopamine) or to prevent the normal recycling of these brain chemicals, which is needed to shut off the signaling between neurons. The result is a brain awash in dopamine, a neurotransmitter present in brain regions that control movement, emotion, motivation, and feelings of pleasure. The overstimulation of this reward system, which normally responds to natural behaviors linked to survival (eating, spending time with loved ones, etc.), produces euphoric effects in response to psychoactive drugs. This reaction sets in motion a reinforcing pattern that "teaches" people to repeat the rewarding behavior of abusing drugs.

As a person continues to abuse drugs, the brain adapts to the overwhelming surges in dopamine by producing less dopamine or by reducing the number of dopamine receptors in the reward circuit. The result is a lessening of dopamine's impact on the reward circuit, which reduces the abuser's ability to enjoy the drugs, as well as the events in life that previously brought pleasure. This decrease compels the addicted person to keep abusing drugs in an attempt to bring the dopamine function back to normal, except now larger amounts of the drug are required to achieve the same dopamine high—an effect known as tolerance.

Long-term abuse causes changes in other brain chemical systems and circuits as well. Glutamate is a neurotransmitter that influences the reward circuit and the ability to learn. When the optimal concentration of glutamate is altered by drug abuse, the brain attempts to compensate, which can impair cognitive function. Brain imaging studies of drug-addicted individuals show changes in areas of the brain that are critical to judgment, decision making, learning and memory, and behavior control. Together, these changes can drive an abuser to seek out and take drugs compulsively despite adverse, even devastating consequences—that is the nature of addiction.

A Combination of Factors

No single factor can predict whether a person will become addicted to drugs. Risk for addiction is influenced by a combination of factors that include individual biology, social environment, and age or stage of development. The more risk factors an individual has, the greater the chance that taking drugs can lead to addiction. For example:

- *Biology*. The genes that people are born with—in combination with environmental influences—account for about half of their addiction vulnerability. Additionally, gender, ethnicity, and the presence of other mental disorders may influence risk for drug abuse and addiction.

- *Environment*. A person's environment includes many different influences, from family and friends to socioeconomic status and quality of life in general. Factors such as peer pressure, physical and sexual abuse, stress, and quality of parenting can greatly influence the occurrence of drug abuse and the escalation to addiction in a person's life.

- *Development*. Genetic and environmental factors interact with critical developmental stages in a person's life to affect addiction vulnerability. Although taking drugs at any age can lead to addiction, the earlier that drug use begins, the more likely it will progress to more serious abuse, which poses a special challenge to adolescents. Because their brains are still developing in the areas that govern decisionmaking, judgment, and self-control, adolescents may be especially prone to risk-taking behaviors, including trying drugs of abuse.

Prevention Is the Key

Drug addiction is a preventable disease. Results from NIDA-funded research have shown that prevention programs involving families, schools, communities, and the media are effective in reducing drug abuse. Although many events and cultural factors affect drug abuse trends, when youths perceive drug abuse as harmful, they reduce their drug taking. Thus, education and outreach are key in helping youth and the general public understand the risks of drug abuse. Teachers, parents, medical and public health professionals must keep sending the message that drug addiction can be prevented if one never abuses drugs.

| *"Addiction is not as hopeless or uncontrollable as the brain disease metaphor suggests."*

Drug Addiction Is Not a Brain Disease

Sally Satel and Scott Lilienfeld

Sally Satel is a psychiatrist at Oasis Clinic in Washington, DC, and a resident scholar at American Enterprise Institute. Scott Lilienfeld is a professor of psychology at Emory University. In the following viewpoint Satel and Lilienfeld challenge recent efforts by Congress and federal agencies to redefine drug and alcohol addiction as brain diseases. The view that addiction is the result of personal choices is preferable, the authors argue, because it is less fatalistic and because it more accurately assumes the ability of individuals to make changes in their behavior that can lead to health rather than accepting passively that they "have" a disease.

As you read, consider the following questions:

1. What do the authors mean that the concept of addiction as a brain disease is "bad for the public's mental health literacy"?

2. What is relapse prevention therapy, according to Satel and Lilienfeld?
3. What conclusions, according to the authors, have been drawn from images of brains under the influence of drugs and alcohol?

A full-scale campaign is under way to change the public perception of drug addiction, from a moral failing to a brain disease. Last spring [2007], HBO aired an ambitious series that touted addiction as a "chronic and relapsing brain disease." In early July, a *Time* magazine cover story suggested that addiction is the doing of the neurotransmitter dopamine, which courses through the brain's reward circuits. And now Congress is weighing in.

A new bill sponsored by Sen. Joe Biden, D-Del., would change the name of the National Institute on Drug Abuse [NIDA] to the National Institute on Diseases of Addiction and change the name of the National Institute on Alcohol Abuse and Alcoholism to the National Institute on Alcohol Disorders and Health. Called the Recognizing Addiction as a Disease Act of 2007, it explains, "The pejorative term 'abuse' used in connection with diseases of addiction has the adverse effect of increasing social stigma and personal shame, both of which are so often barriers to an individual's decision to seek treatment." Addiction should be known as a brain disease, the bill proclaims, "because drugs change the brain's structure and manner in which it functions. These brain changes can be long lasting, and can lead to the harmful behaviors seen in people who abuse drugs."

Good Intentions, Bad Outcome
As a psychiatrist who treats heroin addicts and a psychologist long interested in the philosophical meaning of disease, we have chafed at the "brain disease" rhetoric since it was first promulgated by NIDA in 1995. Granted, the rationale behind it is well-intentioned. Nevertheless, we believe that the brain disease concept is bad for the public's mental health literacy.

Characterizing addiction as a brain disease misappropriates language more properly used to describe conditions such as multiple sclerosis or schizophrenia—afflictions that are neither brought on by sufferers themselves nor modifiable by their desire to be well. Also, the brain disease rhetoric is fatalistic, implying that users can never fully free themselves of their drug or alcohol problems. Finally, and most important, it threatens to obscure the vast role personal agency plays in perpetuating the cycle of use and relapse to drugs and alcohol.

It is true that a cocaine addict in the throes of a days-long binge or a junkie doubled over in misery from withdrawal can't reasonably be expected to get up and walk away.

Yet addicts rarely spend all of their time in the throes of an intense neurochemical siege. In the days between binges, cocaine addicts make many decisions that have nothing to do with drug-seeking. Should they try to find a different job? Kick that freeloading cousin off their couch for good? Register for food stamps? Most of the patients one of us treats hold jobs while pursuing their heroin habits.

What About Better Choices?

In other words, there is room for other choices. These addicts could go to a Narcotics Anonymous meeting, enter treatment if they have private insurance, or register at a public clinic if they don't. Self-governance, in fact, is key to the most promising treatments for addiction. For example, relapse prevention therapy helps patients identify cues—often people, places, and things—that reliably trigger a burst of desire to use. Patients rehearse strategies for avoiding the cues if they possibly can and managing the craving when they cannot. In drug courts (a jail-diversion treatment program for nonviolent drug offenders), offenders are sanctioned for continued drug use (perhaps a night or two in jail) and rewarded for cooperation with the program. The judge holds the person, not his brain, accountable for setbacks and progress.

The brave new world of brain scanning figures prominently in the new disease rhetoric. During imaging experiments in which an addict is shown drug paraphernalia, the reward centers in his brain light up like a Christmas tree. It's easy to be misled into believing that these colorful images prove that the addict is helpless to change his behavior. In a powerful experiment, Deena Weisberg, a doctoral candidate at Yale University, and her colleagues presented nonexperts with flawed explanations for psychological phenomena. They were adept at spotting the errors—until, that is, these explanations were accompanied by "Brain scans indicate . . . " With those three words, Weisberg's participants suddenly found the flawed explanations compelling. Yet in truth, at least at this stage of the technology, we rarely learn as much by visualizing addicts' brains than by asking them what they are experiencing and what they desire.

Telling the public that addiction is a "chronic and relapsing brain disease" suggests that an addict's disembodied brain holds the secrets to understanding and helping him. It implies that medication is necessary and that interventions must be applied directly at the level of the brain. But that's not how people recover. For actress Jamie Lee Curtis, for example, quitting painkillers was a spiritual matter. When she appeared on *Larry King Live* recently, the guest host asked her, "What made you get clean?" She responded, "Well, you know what, that turning point was a—was really a moment between me and God. I never went to treatment. I walked into the door of a 12-step program and I have not walked out since."

Shame Can Be Helpful

Finally, dare we ask: Why is stigma bad? It is surely unfortunate if it keeps people from getting help (although we believe the real issue is not embarrassment but fear of a breach of confidentiality). The push to destigmatize overlooks the healthy role that shame can play, by motivating many otherwise reluctant people to seek treatment in the first place and jolting others into quitting before they spiral down too far.

You would think Congress has better things to do than legislate name changes. And in the long run, the well-meaning effort to overmedicalize addiction could have baleful consequences. Addiction is not as hopeless or uncontrollable as the brain disease metaphor suggests. Yes, like other bad habits, it is in our brains—but like other bad habits, it can be broken.

Periodical and Internet Sources Bibliography

The following articles have been selected to supplement the diverse views presented in this chapter.

Tresa Baldas	"Detroit Feeding OxyContin Addiction; Supply Runs Down I-75," *Detroit Free Press*, June 28, 2011.
Deborah Brauser	"Elderly Are Society's 'Invisible Addicts,' Report Says," Medscape News, July 1, 2011. www.medscape.com.
Meredith Canales	"Doctors Warn of Prescription Drug Abuse Dangers," *San Antonio (TX) Express-News*, July 7, 2011.
Bruce Fessier	"Ford Helped Pioneer Addiction Treatment," *USA Today*, July 9, 2011.
Barry Meier and Abby Goodnough	"Administration Wants Tighter Painkiller Rules," *New York Times*, April 19, 2011.
Paula J. Owen	"Teen Abuse of Pills Rises: Drugs May Be Easily Found," *Worcester (MA) Telegram and Gazette*, June 26, 2011.
Alice Park	"Teens and Drugs: Rite of Passage or Recipe for Addiction?," *Time*, June 29, 2011.
Stanton Peele	"Are Addiction and Mental Illness Really Brain Diseases?," *Huffington Post*, June 16, 2011.
Mary Shedden	"Are Americans Addicted to Addiction?," *Tampa (FL) Tribune*, June 29, 2011.
US News & World Report	"Addiction Starts Early in American Society, Report Finds," June 29, 2011.
Josh Voorhees	"Harry Potter Star Admits to Alcohol Struggles," *Slate*, July 5, 2011.

OPPOSING
VIEWPOINTS®
SERIES

CHAPTER 2

Is Intervention the Best Approach to Addiction?

Chapter Preface

The practice of staging an intervention is sometimes called the Johnson method, after the person who is credited with the early development of the concept. Vernon E. Johnson was an Episcopal priest and self-described alcoholic who successfully overcame his drinking problem and went on, in the early 1960s, to develop a therapeutic approach to chemical dependency that relied heavily on the involvement of family and friends to get the addicted person into treatment. In 1980, after two decades of experience in the field, Johnson published *I'll Quit Tomorrow: A Practical Guide to Alcoholism Treatment*, a book that drew praise for its clear explanation of the physical and emotional changes that accompany the development of addiction and also for its practical suggestions on how to help individuals confront and come to terms with their substance abuse problems. In 1986 Johnson published a second book, *Intervention: A Step-by-Step Guide for Families and Friends of Chemically Dependent Persons*, that is still widely viewed as the classic handbook for those preparing to participate in an intervention.

"You are reading this book because you suspect that someone you care about is chemically dependent," Johnson wrote in the introduction to *Intervention*.

> That someone may be a spouse or a child, a parent or a cousin, a coworker or a neighbor or a friend. The drug of choice may be alcohol, marijuana, cocaine, amphetamines . . . , barbiturates . . . , or a combination of these. What it is does not matter; what matters is that the person is abusing or misusing it, and that this is causing problems for him or her *and for you*.

According to Johnson, family members and friends of alcoholics and addicts have the ability to play an important role in their recovery, both because they care about the individuals involved and because their own lives are often negatively impacted by the addict's behavior. But in order for family members and friends to become forces for constructive change, they need to understand that addiction is a disease process, and to know something about the physical and emotional nature of chemical dependency, which is characterized by a nearly irresistible compulsion to drink or use drugs. In *Intervention: A Step-by-Step Guide for Families and Friends of Chemically Dependent Persons*, Johnson explains that the reason interventions are necessary is because addiction is almost inevitably accompanied by the addict's denial that there is a problem: "Most people, when they come down with a disease, will set about trying to find treatment for it," Johnson wrote. "Here is where chemical dependency distinguishes itself. . . . Chemical dependency is universally accompanied by an emotional syndrome that . . . effectively blocks the consciousness that it exists." The addict's friends and family can help to set a movement toward recovery in motion by addressing the addict's denial head-on, joining forces to name the problem, and then keeping the focus on the addiction long enough to get the person into treatment.

Some critics of interventions that are modeled on the Johnson method argue that confrontation involving multiple parties can be traumatic, not only for those who are addicted, but for others as well, and that emotionally fragile individuals who receive ultimatums can feel that they are being ganged up on or pushed into a corner without real possibility of success. Others say the cost of interventions is too high, and that if general health care and treatment for addicts were more widely available, interventions of this type would not be necessary. These are some of the issues that are examined in this chapter.

> "Research about the success of competing approaches to intervention is not definitive."

Experts Differ on Which Intervention Models Are Most Effective

Sarah Kershaw

Sarah Kershaw is an award-winning reporter who has written for the New York Times *since 2000. In this viewpoint Kershaw discusses the deaths of singers Michael Jackson and Kurt Cobain; Jackson from a drug overdose and Cobain by suicide. Both had abused drugs and both faced interventions to go into treatment, Kershaw asserts. Some models for intervention, the author notes, like those featured on the A&E reality show* Intervention *depend on surprise and ultimatum, while other approaches rely more on counseling and persuasion. Kershaw concludes that while experts agree that it is important to help addicts to understand the consequences of their behavior, they do not agree on the effectiveness of various intervention models.*

As you read, consider the following questions:

1. What do experts say about the role of denial in drug addiction, according to Kershaw?

2. What is a "living room ambush," and why do some believe it is the most effective approach to confronting addiction, as stated by the author?

3. How much do substance abuse interventions cost, according to Kershaw?

In the days following [pop singer] Michael Jackson's death, people close to him said they had warned his family and pleaded with him to get help for drug problems, angrily decrying a coterie of enablers surrounding the star.

Authorities looking into his death now say they believe Mr. Jackson, who in 1993 was treated for a painkiller addiction, had prescriptions written under more than a dozen assumed names.

"He was surrounded by enablers, including a shameful plethora of M.D.'s in Los Angeles and elsewhere who supplied him with prescription drugs," Deepak Chopra, the high-profile spiritual guru and a friend of Mr. Jackson's, wrote on the *Huffington Post* Web site on June 26, [2009,] shortly after the singer's death. "As many times as he would candidly confess that he had a problem" to Dr. Chopra, he wrote, "the conversation always ended with a deflection and denial."

A Lost Opportunity

Specialists in drug interventions—a rapidly growing field since the concept was developed in the late 1960s—have watched the Jackson case closely, viewing it as a classic example of lost opportunity. Denial is at the core of addiction, and breaking through it, many experts say, can require extreme measures, particularly with celebrities, who can procure an endless supply of drugs and are cocooned by people with an interest in keeping the star's earnings flowing.

Whether Mr. Jackson was addicted has not been established, but investigators are proceeding under the assumption that drug abuse was involved. They are pursuing a homicide case against his personal physician, [Conrad Murray,] who reportedly administered a dose of a powerful anesthetic, propofol, before he died. The drug is sometimes used for sleep by painkiller addicts, experts say. [Murray was found guilty of involuntary manslaughter in November 2011.]

Mr. Jackson's biographer, J. Randy Taraborelli, who knew him for 40 years, said in an interview that family members had made attempts at interventions in recent years. Another source close to the family confirmed there were two attempts.

The most common form of intervention, known colloquially as a "living room ambush," relies on surprise and an ultimatum. The addict is lured to a meeting with a promise like "Grandma has a check to give you this Sunday." Bags are packed for a stay in a treatment center, and the family is encouraged to draw the line in unison: get clean and sober, or get out.

This approach is also called the Johnson method, named for an Episcopal priest, Vernon E. Johnson, whose seminal book, "I'll Quit Tomorrow," gave rise to the belief that family and friends, aided by a professional interventionist, could break through the alcoholic or addict's denial. It was intended to avert disaster before an addict hit rock bottom or died, although it has drawn criticism for doing more harm than good, and since the early 1990s, less draconian methods have arisen.

Some experts now caustically refer to traditional intervention as the "A&E model," a reference to the popular reality show *Intervention*, which profiles families and addicts and which always ends with a surprise confrontation.

Showdowns Can Be Traumatic

But critics say such a showdown can add more trauma to already devastated families and addicts, and deter an addict from getting help.

Just as Mr. Jackson's death has highlighted the difficulty of trying to help a chronic drug abuser, it was the death of another

Millions Are Addicted to Pain Killers

The 2009 National Survey on Drug Use and Health found that nearly two million Americans were dependent on or abusing prescription pain relievers—nearly twice as great as the number of people addicted to cocaine. According to the latest statistics compiled by the Centers for Disease Control and Prevention, in 2007 painkillers killed twice as many people as cocaine and five times as many as heroin.

Harvard Health Publications, *January 2011. www.health.harvard.edu.*

celebrity, Kurt Cobain in 1994, that added momentum to an alternative philosophy of intervention known as "motivational interviewing" or "invitational" intervention.

Mr. Cobain, a heroin addict, committed suicide days after disappearing from a rehab center he had agreed to enter after a classic tough-love intervention staged by his wife, Courtney Love, and his Nirvana bandmates, according to news accounts at the time.

It prompted concerns about all-or-nothing interventions among psychologists and addiction experts, according to G. Alan Marlatt, director of the Addictive Behaviors Research Center at the University of Washington. Dr. Marlatt said he spoke with a record label executive who was present at Mr. Cobain's intervention, who recounted that the musician asked friends and family if he could meet them "half way" and cut down on his heroin use, rather than stopping entirely. The answer was no.

It is unlikely there was a single cause for Mr. Cobain's suicide. But it has spurred Dr. Marlatt and others to speak out in support of nonconfrontational approaches. "Many people are unwilling to maintain abstinence, but what are you going to do, wait until they hit bottom, if they even survive?" he said. "Everything is all or none, you're either using or not using, there's no safe middle way from that perspective."

Gentler Approaches

"Motivational interviewing" and other less confrontational approaches involve asking an addict to join family members, who may attend lengthy counseling before and after the encounter with the addict. The family does not necessarily demand that an addict or alcoholic quit using or drinking; they may be asked to cut down their use—part of a treatment known as "harm reduction," which is itself controversial.

"I guess motivational interviewing is not going to be the next reality TV show because it's so boring," said Jeffrey Foote, a founder and the executive director of the Center for Motivation and Change, a treatment and research center in New York. "It's nuanced, it's gentler, it's working with people in a slower way, and it's effective. But that's not good TV. What's good TV is taking drug addicts, harnessing the anger people feel toward addiction and drug addicts, and smashing them in the face."

To traditional interventionists and critics of harm reduction—including 12-step programs, which call for total abstinence—many addicts are both unable to control their intake and stubbornly resistant to getting help unless the consequences are incredibly dire, such as being cut off financially, divorced or faced with jail.

"I have never had anyone call me or e-mail me to say they wished they wouldn't have given someone an ultimatum," said Jeff VanVonderen, one of the three interventionists on the A&E show, who has worked in the field for 25 years and is certified by the state of Illinois to work as an interventionist. "But I have a couple of dozen times had some contact me to tell me that they wish they wouldn't have backed down or waited, because now the person is dead."

Mr. VanVonderen said that of the 137 interventions filmed for the show so far, 135 of the subjects agreed to go to treatment, and 111 are currently sober.

Waiting Can Be Risky

He and other interventionists agree that Al-Anon, the popular 12-step program for the families of alcoholics and addicts, which holds that relatives should "detach with love" because an addict will only seek help at rock bottom, is a powerful support but that waiting for that bottom risks lives.

Research about the success of competing approaches to intervention is not definitive, in part because the data on recovery is unreliable: why an addict stays sober or relapses is hard to measure. But some studies on the nonconfrontational approaches, described by independent researchers not doing the interventions themselves as statistically sound, have shown the Johnson model to be both less effective in getting an addict into treatment and linked to higher relapse rates, compared with softer approaches, including one called "carefrontation."

Interventions of any kind can be costly, ranging from $1,500 to $15,000, depending on the interventionist and whether travel is involved, said Corinne Butler-Williams, president of the National Association of Drug and Alcohol Interventionists, which she founded in 1985. She could not estimate the number of working interventionists because they do not need to be certified by state boards or her own association to practice. But her group is certifying a growing number, she said, and interest in the field has exploded because of the A&E show.

Tough Love Can Drive Change

Most interventionists agree that no matter the approach, an addict has to be made aware of the enormous consequences of his addiction and behavior. Drug courts, which give nonviolent substance abusers the option of undergoing treatment rather than going to jail, have spread across the country in the last two decades—and they certainly espouse a philosophy of tough love.

R. Gil Kerlikowske, who in May [2009] was sworn in as the [Barack] Obama administration's director of the Office of National Drug Control Policy, is a supporter of drug courts as an alternative to mandatory drug sentencing. The new drug czar and the man nominated as his deputy, A. Thomas McLellan, are viewed by many addiction experts as representative of a sea change in thinking about treatment: away from the punitive, toward more acceptance of nuances and complications of addiction.

"Ten years ago, if you would have asked me this question about addiction, I would have said it's obviously a moral failure and I don't know why people can't pull themselves up from their bootstraps and handle this and get themselves totally clean," Mr. Kerlikowske, a former police chief in Seattle, said in an interview. "But we can be going in a different direction. We can look at this from different viewpoints now."

One of the newest alternatives to the Johnson model, developed by Brad Lamm, a New York City interventionist, relies heavily on technology like Skype, podcasts and Internet chatting to connect families with addicts in an effort to include as many significant friends and relatives as possible, far flung as they may be.

Ideally, he said, the families continue to "meet" as a group weekly while the addict is in treatment and for up to six months after that. He makes podcasts of the meetings so both family members and addicts can revisit the meetings, as a reminder that they are all in it together, he said.

"The thinking was that the addict needs to be captured, then once captured needs to be treated," Mr. Lamm said. "But what I know from working with families is that we can use the family strength to get us where we want to go, to healthier relationships, even in the face of crushing addiction."

| "Whether [intervention] will work here [in the UK], or not, is too early to say."

The American Model of Intervention May Not Be the Best Approach in Other Countries

Emine Saner

In this viewpoint Emine Saner, a feature writer for the Guardian, *a British newspaper, contrasts the British and American approaches to substance abuse intervention. Formal interventions are more common in the United States, Saner argues, due in part to the popular reality television show* Intervention. *In the United Kingdom, treatment for substance abuse problems is available through the National Health Service, the author notes, and contends that the model used in America may or may not work in the UK.*

As you read, consider the following questions:

1. What are some of the techniques Saner cites John Southworth as mentioning that make addicts "thirsty"?
2. How much does it cost to enter into an NHS drug treatment program, according to the author?

3. According to Saner, how long does it typically take to be
   admitted to a drug treatment program in England?

Around 50 people gathered [in October 2010] in a small conference room in a hotel in west London to hear two former
drug addicts speak. John Southworth and Ken Seeley both run
their own interventionist companies in the US and [were] here
to train people in the tactic—effectively, taking a person with
an addiction (drugs, alcohol, gambling or any kind of compulsive behaviour) and putting them in a residential rehabilitation
centre.

Interventions have a higher profile in America ("The UK
[United Kingdom] is going through what the US did many years
ago," says Southworth), largely thanks to a reality television show
called *Intervention*, in which Seeley starred. Last year [2009],
the series won an Emmy award but it has also been criticised
for exploiting vulnerable people, because the tactics Seeley and
Southworth describe are so tough—people have been thrown out
on the street to see how they cope once their family are encouraged to stop "enabling" their addiction; others are chased by the
camera as they try to run away.

Techniques for Building Motivation

"You can lead a horse to water but you can't make it drink," says
Southworth, "but we can make it damn thirsty. It's about creating
consequences." This can be anything from threatening a person
who has stolen from their family with reporting them to the police, or making them realise that without getting help for their
addiction they could lose a professional licence (if, for example,
the person is a pilot, or a nurse). "Our job is to work out what
is going to be the consequences that will get them thirsty," says
Southworth.

"I had [a client] who waited three days. She slept in the
street," says Seeley. Doesn't it worry them that vulnerable people
are being put in a potentially dangerous situation? "Yes," says

UK Drug Treatment Statistics

- 206,889 individuals aged 18 and over were recorded as in contact with structured drug treatment services in England in 2009/10. . . .

- 192,367 individuals (93%) were effectively engaged in treatment for 12 weeks or more, or if leaving treatment before 12 weeks did so free of dependency. . . .

- Of the 77,374 individuals who commenced their first structured treatment intervention in 2009/10, 73,059 (94%) waited 3 weeks or less.

National Drug Treatment Monitoring System, 2010. www.nta.nhs.uk.

Southworth, "but if nothing else works, what are you going to do? It's called tough love." If they believe someone is genuinely in danger, says Seeley, "we have police checking on them, or a private investigator or interventionist in visual contact with them."

In the UK, there are relatively few professional interventionists. Bill Stevens, a former addictions counsellor for the Priory group of hospitals, set up his company Red Chair two years ago [2008] and feels that "it is bound to grow". Stevens has carried out around 45 interventions. Would he advise a family to throw the person with an addiction out on the street? "An intervention should be based on love and dignity. Why chuck a sick person out on the street? I think the idea of intervention being aggressive . . . it should be the opposite."

Referral Fees Raise Ethical Issues

One of the main aims of the conference, he says, was to set up a self-regulating body in the UK. There are people, he says, who work on a type of commission, paid by private treatment centres to essentially feed patients to them. "If you are paid a referral fee then you are in a huge ethical dilemma," he says, adding that Red Chair charges the family for the intervention—usually around £750 [about $1240]—not the treatment centre.

"A family member will ring up and say their loved one has a drug or alcohol problem and I'll work through the pre-intervention screening process: is it right to do something, who is affected, what are the consequences, what will happen if you do nothing? It's about treating the family as well, so they can help someone go to treatment and then support the person after treatment."

Then he will often bring the family together with the person and ask them to go into treatment. Faced with that, he says, very few refuse. In most cases, the person is treated privately, but for those who can't afford it, Stevens assists them to go through the NHS [National Health Service] process.

Paying for an intervention is partly what worries Andrew Horne, director of operations in Scotland for the addiction charity Addaction. "Every single person in the country has the right to an NHS community care assessment," he says. "From that, they will assess what those needs are and devise a care plan. I have a little bit of concern around interventionists in that I know people who have paid for residential private care when really they couldn't afford it, but they did it because they felt they were desperate. They didn't know they could have got that for free. [Intervention] is very much an American model because of the American healthcare system, which is pay as you go."

If there is a fault in the system, he says, it is in not making people aware there is help out there. "In England the system is fast—the target is to go from referral to treatment in three weeks." (Scotland is a little behind that.) But don't people use interventionists as a last resort? "The idea of working with involuntary clients is not alien to most drug charities and treatment systems," he says.

Horne is also concerned about the reliance on residential treatment. "There are fantastic services in the community and while people like residential care because it gives a certain amount of safety, the efficacy of that care is sometimes not as good as if they remained in the community. Placing someone in residential care means they still have to return to their lives."

A vast proportion of interventionists are former addicts themselves. Stevens went into treatment for his addiction 17 years ago. Seeley was addicted to crystal meth, Southworth to cocaine; both have been clean for more than 20 years. "I'm in recovery. I've been there," says Southworth. "An addict can't lie to another addict. They know we've been there. I don't want people to go [through] what I did—jail, job loss, family loss." Many interventionists are fuelled, he says, by a desire not to allow other people's lives to be ruined by addiction. Whether it will work here, or not, is too early to say.

| "There is evidence for harm reduction interventions that . . . definitely work—such as methadone and other replacement therapies, or needle and syringe programmes."

Harm Reduction Is the Best Approach When Addicts Will Not Quit Using

Tim Morrison

Tim Morrison, author of The Essential Drug and Alcohol Worker, *develops training programs for people who work with drug users in the United Kingdom. In this viewpoint he describes harm reduction, a set of strategies for minimizing the negative consequences of habitual drug use. Harm reduction was adopted in the 1980s, when HIV/AIDS first appeared among gay men and drug users in the United Kingdom. Morrison contends that it is the best treatment model for drug users who are unwilling or unable to stop using.*

As you read, consider the following questions:

1. What are some of the harm reduction practices that are listed by the author?

2. Why has harm reduction been a controversial policy in the United Kingdom, according to Hunt?

3. The author cites evidence on needle exchange programs that shows what?

Harm reduction is concerned with minimising the negative impact of drugs and alcohol on individuals and communities. The need to help prevent harm to the health and lifestyle of the individual user as well as to the people around him or her is seen to be paramount.

It is a pragmatic group of strategies that recognises that many people are either not ready or are unwilling to cease their drug use. Harm reduction means that no matter how people feel about their drug use there are practical services that can be offered to them.

This means that people can be brought into contact with sources of assistance early on in their drug using careers. If people do not want to stop taking drugs then

• advice about how to use drugs more safely will be provided

• they may be offered some drug using equipment

• for some there may be prescribable alternatives to illegal sources of supply. . . .

Rationale Behind Harm Reduction

In the 1980s when HIV first appeared in the United Kingdom there was very considerable and justifiable anxiety about what the impact would be on groups disproportionately affected by it and on the wider population. Particular concern was raised by the devastating effect of the virus on some drug using communities particularly in Edinburgh.

The [Margaret] Thatcher Government decided to accept a pragmatic response to strategies targeted by groups who were

Harm Reduction

Harm reduction targets the causes of risks and harms. The identification of specific harms, their causes, and decisions about appropriate interventions requires proper assessment of the problem and the actions needed. The tailoring of harm reduction interventions to address the specific risks and harms must also take into account factors which may render people who use drugs particularly vulnerable, such as age, gender and incarceration.

Harm Reduction International, 2011.
www.ihra.net.

then seen to be most at risk—then men who have sex with men and injecting drug users.

This decision was at the time very controversial—many argued that this meant that the State was effectively colluding in a range of anti-social behaviours and enabling them to continue. The rationale behind harm reduction was summarised by the Advisory Council on the Misuse of Drugs [ACMD]: 'HIV is a greater threat to public and individual health than drug misuse. The first goal of work with drug users must therefore be to prevent them from acquiring or transmitting the virus. In some cases this will be achieved through abstinence. In others, abstinence will not be achievable for the time being and efforts will have to focus on risk reduction. Abstinence remains the ultimate goal but efforts to bring it about in individual cases must not jeopardise any reduction in HIV risk behaviour which has already been achieved.'

The ACMD recognised that people would not stop taking drugs because they were being told not to do it—that 'Just Say

No' strategies may deter some people from taking drugs but they would have minimal impact on the community of people who were injecting.

Accepting this—the question then became one of how people could be engaged with services so that lives could be saved—that people could be kept alive long enough to get into treatment.

For this to happen, clean injecting equipment had to be made widely available and people had to be taught how to use it—hence the first needle exchanges.

Although the spread of HIV has to a certain extent been contained amongst injecting drug users, the need for needle exchanges continues—this has been emphasised by the emergence of a new and potentially devastating blood borne virus—Hepatitis C.

Achievements of the Model

Professor Gary Stimson in a speech to the Methadone Alliance Conference in 2000 argued for three major achievements of harm reduction: "We were ahead of many countries in the prescribing of substitute opiate drugs to people who are dependent on them—a history which goes back to the 1920s, to a time when the UK and the US started on very different drugs policy paths. HIV prevention has been a remarkable success story in the UK. We were looked to in admiration by many others around the world. It is a success that has the potential to be repeated, with respect to HCV and HBV [hepatitis viruses C and B, respectively]. We also managed to develop effective harm reduction measures associated with the consumption of other drugs." . . .

There are many opponents of harm reduction strategies who argue that they simply collude with harmful drug use and make it harder for people to give up [using drugs]. Melanie Phillips, the journalist, is perhaps the best known opponent of harm reduction in Britain—she argues that it is 'actually a euphemism for throwing in the towel altogether against drug abuse'.

Harm Reduction Works

In 1997, in Connecticut, a needle exchange caused a great deal of hostility in the surrounding community due to discarded syringes and so on. The exchange was closed down forcing people to use more risky methods of using but the levels of drug related debris did not decrease.

One 2001 literature review reported that "despite variations between programs, a recent international comparison showed that in 29 cities with established NEPs [needle exchange programs], HIV prevalence decreased on average by 5.8% per year, but it increased on average by 5.9% per year in 51 cities without NEPs".

Neil Hunt in his review of the evidence bases argues that there is evidence for harm reduction interventions that:

• definitely work—such as methadone and other replacement therapies, or needle and syringe programmes. These should be considered for adoption in regions where they are currently unavailable;

• show promise and require cautious expansion with evaluation in ways that are adapted to local settings, e.g. heroin prescribing, depenalisation, the use of drug consumption rooms and pill testing;

• are widely used yet under-researched—notably information, education and communication programmes and motivational interviewing approaches to conventional harm reduction targets such as the prevention of HIV, hepatitis C, hepatitis B and overdose.

Harm Reduction for the Community

Since the advent of [the] New Labour [Party to power in the UK], the association between drugs and crime has become much more fixed in the mind of Government and the popular press. This has paved the way for rhetoric around reducing harms to communities and here the target is reducing crime and in particular, theft and certain crimes of violence. Much of the official language justifying the prescribing of substitute opiates (methadone and Subutex) specifically talks about it being an investment that pays back in terms of reduced loss to the economy.

> "In 2007 . . . 20.8 million persons
> (8.4 percent of the population aged 12
> or older) needed treatment for an illicit
> drug or alcohol use problem but did not
> receive it."

Drug and Alcohol Addictions Often Go Untreated

National Institute on Drug Abuse

This viewpoint from the National Institute on Drug Abuse (NIDA) describes addiction as a chronic illness, characterized by intense and uncontrollable craving, that affected more than 23 million people in 2007. Only a small percentage of the individuals that need treatment receive it. This is true in spite of the fact that a number of effective treatment options are available.

As you read, consider the following questions:

1. How many people in the United States received treatment for a drug or alcohol addiction in 2007, according to NIDA?
2. According to the author, why is medically assisted detoxification viewed as only the first step in treatment?

3. What medications does NIDA list that have been found to be helpful to users of opioids, tobacco, and alcohol?

Drug addiction is a complex illness characterized by intense and, at times, uncontrollable drug craving, along with compulsive drug seeking and use that persist even in the face of devastating consequences. While the path to drug addiction begins with the voluntary act of taking drugs, over time a person's ability to choose not to do so becomes compromised, and seeking and consuming the drug becomes compulsive. This behavior results largely from the effects of prolonged drug exposure on brain functioning. Addiction is a brain disease that affects multiple brain circuits, including those involved in reward and motivation, learning and memory, and inhibitory control over behavior.

Because drug abuse and addiction have so many dimensions and disrupt so many aspects of an individual's life, treatment is not simple. Effective treatment programs typically incorporate many components, each directed to a particular aspect of the illness and its consequences. Addiction treatment must help the individual stop using drugs, maintain a drug-free lifestyle, and achieve productive functioning in the family, at work, and in society. Because addiction is typically a chronic disease, people cannot simply stop using drugs for a few days and be cured. Most patients require long-term or repeated episodes of care to achieve the ultimate goal of sustained abstinence and recovery of their lives.

Too often, addiction goes untreated: According to SAMHSA's [Substance Abuse and Mental Health Services Administration's] National Survey on Drug Use and Health (NSDUH), 23.2 million persons (9.4 percent of the U.S. population) aged 12 or older needed treatment for an illicit drug or alcohol use problem in 2007. Of these individuals, 2.4 million (10.4 percent of those who needed treatment) received treatment at a specialty facility (i.e., hospital, drug or alcohol rehabilitation or mental health center). Thus, 20.8 million persons (8.4 percent of the population aged 12 or older) needed treatment for an illicit drug or alcohol use problem but did not receive it. These estimates are similar to those in previous years.

Principles of Effective Treatment

Scientific research since the mid-1970s shows that treatment can help patients addicted to drugs stop using, avoid relapse, and successfully recover their lives. Based on this research, key principles have emerged that should form the basis of any effective treatment programs:

- Addiction is a complex but treatable disease that affects brain function and behavior.
- No single treatment is appropriate for everyone.
- Treatment needs to be readily available.
- Effective treatment attends to multiple needs of the individual, not just his or her drug abuse.
- Remaining in treatment for an adequate period of time is critical.
- Counseling—individual and/or group—and other behavioral therapies are the most commonly used forms of drug abuse treatment.
- Medications are an important element of treatment for many patients, especially when combined with counseling and other behavioral therapies.
- An individual's treatment and services plan must be assessed continually and modified as necessary to ensure that it meets his or her changing needs.
- Many drug-addicted individuals also have other mental disorders.
- Medically assisted detoxification is only the first stage of addiction treatment and by itself does little to change long-term drug abuse.

- Treatment does not need to be voluntary to be effective.
- Drug use during treatment must be monitored continuously, as lapses during treatment do occur.
- Treatment programs should assess patients for the presence of HIV/AIDS, hepatitis B and C, tuberculosis, and other infectious diseases as well as provide targeted risk-reduction counseling to help patients modify or change behaviors that place them at risk of contracting or spreading infectious diseases.

Effective Treatment Approaches

Medication and behavioral therapy, especially when combined, are important elements of an overall therapeutic process that often begins with detoxification, followed by treatment and relapse prevention. Easing withdrawal symptoms can be important in the initiation of treatment; preventing relapse is necessary for maintaining its effects. And sometimes, as with other chronic conditions, episodes of relapse may require a return to prior treatment components. A continuum of care that includes a customized treatment regimen—addressing all aspects of an individual's life, including medical and mental health services—and follow-up options (e.g., community—or family-based recovery support systems) can be crucial to a person's success in achieving and maintaining a drug-free lifestyle.

Medications

Medications can be used to help with different aspects of the treatment process.

Withdrawal. Medications offer help in suppressing withdrawal symptoms during detoxification. However, medically assisted detoxification is not in itself "treatment"—it is only the first step in the treatment process. Patients who go through medically assisted withdrawal but do not receive any further treatment

By Drug: Admissions to Publicly Funded Substance Abuse Treatment Programs, 2006

Percentage of Admissions	Substance or Drug
21.9	Alcohol
17.8	Alcohol + another drug
16.1	Marijuana
13.7	Heroin
9.9	Smoked cocaine (crack)
8.7	Stimulants
4.2	Opiates (not heroin)
4.0	Other-than-smoked cocaine (e.g., cocaine powder)
0.4	Tranquilizers
0.2	PCP
0.2	Sedatives
0.1	Hallucinogens
0.1	Inhalants
0.5	Other drugs
2.4	None reported

TAKEN FROM: "NIDA InfoFacts: Treatment Statistics," National Institute on Drug Abuse, June 2008. www.drugabuse.gov.

show drug abuse patterns similar to those who were never treated.

Treatment. Medications can be used to help reestablish normal brain function and to prevent relapse and diminish cravings. Currently, we have medications for opioids (heroin, morphine), tobacco (nicotine), and alcohol addiction and are developing others for treating stimulant (cocaine, methamphetamine) and cannabis (marijuana) addiction. Most people with severe addiction problems, however, are polydrug users (users of more than one drug) and will require treatment for all of the substances that they abuse.

- *Opioids:* Methadone, buprenorphine and, for some individuals, naltrexone are effective medications for the treatment of opiate addiction. Acting on the same targets in the brain as heroin and morphine, methadone and buprenorphine suppress withdrawal symptoms and relieve cravings. Naltrexone works by blocking the effects of heroin or other opioids at their receptor sites and should only be used in patients who have already been detoxified. Because of compliance issues, naltrexone is not as widely used as the other medications. All medications help patients disengage from drug seeking and related criminal behavior and become more receptive to behavioral treatments.

- *Tobacco:* A variety of formulations of nicotine replacement therapies now exist—including the patch, spray, gum, and lozenges—that are available over the counter. In addition, two prescription medications have been FDA-approved for tobacco addiction: bupropion and varenicline. They have different mechanisms of action in the brain, but both help prevent relapse in people trying to quit. Each of the above medications is recommended for use in combination with behavioral treatments, including group and individual therapies, as well as telephone quitlines.

- *Alcohol:* Three medications have been FDA-approved for treating alcohol dependence: naltrexone, acamprosate, and disulfiram. A fourth, topiramate, is showing encouraging results in clinical trials. Naltrexone blocks opioid receptors that are involved in the rewarding effects of drinking and in the craving for alcohol. It reduces relapse to heavy drinking and is highly effective in some but not all patients—this is likely related to genetic differences. Acamprosate is thought to reduce symptoms of protracted withdrawal, such as insomnia, anxiety, restlessness, and dysphoria (an unpleasant or uncomfortable emotional state, such as depression, anxiety, or irritability). It may be more effective in patients with severe dependence. Disulfiram interferes with the degradation of alcohol, resulting in the accumulation of acetaldehyde, which, in turn, produces a very unpleasant reaction that includes flushing, nausea, and palpitations if the patient drinks alcohol. Compliance can be a problem, but among patients who are highly motivated, disulfiram can be very effective.

Behavioral Treatments

Behavioral treatments help patients engage in the treatment process, modify their attitudes and behaviors related to drug abuse, and increase healthy life skills. These treatments can also enhance the effectiveness of medications and help people stay in treatment longer. Treatment for drug abuse and addiction can be delivered in many different settings using a variety of behavioral approaches.

Outpatient behavioral treatment encompasses a wide variety of programs for patients who visit a clinic at regular intervals. Most of the programs involve individual or group drug counseling. Some programs also offer other forms of behavioral treatment such as—

- *Cognitive-behavioral therapy*, which seeks to help patients recognize, avoid, and cope with the situations in which they are most likely to abuse drugs.
- *Multidimensional family therapy*, which was developed for adolescents with drug abuse problems—as well as their families—addresses a range of influences on their drug

abuse patterns and is designed to improve overall family functioning.

• *Motivational interviewing*, which capitalizes on the readiness of individuals to change their behavior and enter treatment.

• *Motivational incentives* (contingency management), which uses positive reinforcement to encourage abstinence from drugs.

Residential treatment programs can also be very effective, especially for those with more severe problems. For example, *therapeutic communities* (TCs) are highly structured programs in which patients remain at a residence, typically for 6 to 12 months. TCs differ from other treatment approaches principally in their use of the community—treatment staff and those in recovery—as a key agent of change to influence patient attitudes, perceptions, and behaviors associated with drug use. Patients in TCs may include those with relatively long histories of drug addiction, involvement in serious criminal activities, and seriously impaired social functioning. TCs are now also being designed to accommodate the needs of women who are pregnant or have children. The focus of the TC is on the resocialization of the patient to a drug-free, crime-free lifestyle.

Treatment While Incarcerated

Treatment in a criminal justice setting can succeed in preventing an offender's return to criminal behavior, particularly when treatment continues as the person transitions back into the community. Studies show that treatment does not need to be voluntary to be effective.

Periodical and Internet Sources Bibliography

The following articles have been selected to supplement the diverse views presented in this chapter.

Neal Conan	"Reassessing Anonymity in 12-Step Programs," National Public Radio, July 7, 2011. www.npr.org.
Daily Mail (London)	"'I Thought It Would Tear Us Apart': Keith Urban Feared Rehab Would Destroy Marriage to Nicole Kidman," November 30, 2010.
Bruce Fessier	"Betty Ford Showed Strength in Admitting Weakness for Alcohol, Pain Medicine," *Desert Sun* (Palm Springs, CA), July 8, 2011.
Caroline Gallay	"A Vaccine for Cocaine Addiction? Baylor's Dr. Kosten Is on the Brink of a Breakthrough for Addicts," *CultureMap Houston*, July 7, 2011.
Elizabeth Landau	"Intervening Against an Adult's Will Is Complicated, Painful," CNN, July 10, 2009. www.cnn.com.
Anthony McCartney	"Betty Ford Helped Pave Road to Recovery for Stars," Associated Press, July 10, 2011. www.ap.org.
Shantal Parris Riley	"Report: Alcohol Is Teen Drug of Choice," *Rochester (NY) Democrat and Chronicle*, June 20, 2011.
Gina Salamone	"Lindsay Lohan's Mom Dina Slams Michael Lohan for Intervention, Drug Abuse Comments," *New York Daily News*, October 19, 2009.
Paula Span	"The Aging Drinker," *New York Times*, April 12, 2010.
Cary Tennis	"My Dad's an Alcoholic and He Won't Stop Drinking," *Salon*, September 7, 2011.
United Press International	"Jackson's Kin Attempted Intervention," July 9, 2009. www.upi.com.

CHAPTER 3

Who Should Be Involved in Substance Abuse Interventions?

Chapter Preface

Viewers of the A&E television series *Intervention* are familiar with Vernon E. Johnson's instructions for forming an intervention team: "Make a list of meaningful persons other than yourself who surround the chemically dependent person," Johnson wrote in *Intervention: How to Help Someone Who Doesn't Want Help* in 1986. "The key term here is *meaningful*. These should be persons with whom the victim has a fairly close relationship, whether by necessity or by choice. They should exert a strong influence upon the victim, since his or her denial will sweep aside the efforts of others."

The role of the intervention team, as Johnson saw it, is to present reality to a person who has—because of his or her use of drugs or alcohol—lost touch with reality, and to do it in a way that the person is able to receive. Although the essential character of an intervention is confrontational, Johnson stressed that it not be judgmental. "In an intervention, confrontation means compelling a person to face the facts about his or her chemical dependency. It is not a punishment. It is not an opportunity for others to clobber him or her verbally. It is an attack upon the victim's wall of defenses, not upon the victim as a person." Johnson emphasized the importance of compassion, rooted in an understanding of the delusional character of addiction, and that it is an illness.

High on Johnson's list of desirable members of an intervention team is the person's spouse, employer or supervisor, parents and siblings. Employers are especially valued as members of an intervention team, because of their ability to break through a person's denial. "Chemical dependents often cling to their job performance as the last bastion of respectability as the disease brings the rest of the world crashing down around their ears," Johnson wrote. "They use it as 'proof' that they can't have a problem."

Other possible team members include close friends and children of the addict or alcoholic who are at least eight years old. The involvement of children is desirable, according to Johnson, because children are often hurt as a result of a parent's drinking or drug problem and because the process of education that goes on in an intervention helps them to understand the nature of the problem and that addiction is an illness. At the same time, becoming aware of a child's suffering can be a powerful wake-up call to a person with a drinking or drug abuse problem.

Vernon Johnson's model for conducting a substance abuse intervention relies heavily on the power of family, friends and employers. However, other individuals, especially health care professionals, are also in a position to intervene, to "present reality to a person who has lost touch with reality," stated Johnson. Who should be involved in substance abuse interventions, and how can they prepare themselves to be more effective in that role? That is the question that is considered in the following chapter.

| "Businesses have an obligation to step in and be more aggressive in addressing addictions in the workplace by intervening more proactively."

Businesses Have an Obligation to Intervene in Cases of Workplace Addiction

Bob Poznanovich

In this viewpoint Bob Poznanovich, the president and CEO of Addiction Intervention Resources, Inc., shares his personal story of becoming addicted to cocaine. His point is to argue that workplaces have an important role to play in addressing substance abuse problems.

As you read, consider the following questions:

1. Why does the author believe his company and coworkers would have been successful in persuading him to go into treatment for his drug problem?
2. What are some of the things Poznanovich says companies can do to address the problem of substance abuse in the workplace?

Bob Poznanovich, "Perspectives: A Personal Story of Addiction at Work," *Behavioral Healthcare*, July 2006. Behavioral.net. Copyright © 2006 by *Behavioral Healthcare*. All rights reserved. Reproduced by permission.

3. What happened when the author discovered that one of his employees had begun using drugs again?

As a young man I was very career-motivated and was rewarded with success quickly. By the time I was 30 years old, I was vice-president of sales for Zenith Data Systems, a billion-dollar subsidiary of Zenith Electronics Corp. I was in charge of hundreds of employees and hundreds of millions of dollars in revenue. I was on top of my career and had the world in my hands, but I forgot all of the lessons I learned growing up on the streets in Chicago—that bad things happen to people who do drugs.

I remember one evening in particular when I was at a party in an exclusive Gold Coast neighborhood in downtown Chicago and someone introduced me to cocaine. It was the mid-1980s and I had heard about cocaine; it was the drug of the rich and famous. I wanted to be rich and famous, too. I had made it, I was a corporate executive, and so were these people. So I tried cocaine, and I loved it and its effect. It maximized my strengths and minimized my weaknesses (or so I thought at the time). I was addicted immediately, but it would take years and the loss of my fiancée, my job, and almost my life before I realized that I had a problem.

It's difficult to look back and remember the effect my drug use had on my company, employees, customers, friends, and family. These people respected me, and I let everyone down. Obviously this was a destructive time for my family and me, along with the company and its employees and customers. The sad part for them, and for me, was that nobody was able to help. Not only was I in denial about my addiction, but most of my coworkers were in denial, as well. What's worse, those who weren't in denial didn't know what to do.

I learned many years later that there were many meetings at work *about* me but never a meeting *with* me. The result was that my addiction continued to grow, and I ultimately lost my job and everything else that was important to me.

Where Did They Go Wrong?

Looking back at that point in my life, it became clear to me that if the company had stepped in and talked to me, had done some form of intervention early on, I would have gotten help immediately. I would have gone to treatment, and I would have stopped using drugs. Work and my career were so important that I would have done anything to save them. But instead I thought that I had it under control, that I would be able to quit drugs on my own. "I'll quit tomorrow," I would say to myself—but tomorrow never came. Fortunately, I was able to get to treatment several years after I was fired; *unfortunately*, I had to lose almost everything before I was willing to get help.

I know that my story is similar to many in business today, and I know that many companies and employees are making the same mistakes. Most companies have a drug-free workplace policy and some form of EAP; these are steps in the right direction, but we need to do more. Companies need to be more proactive to face addictions and other compulsive behaviors in the workplace. They need to create environments where employees and managers are trained on how to identify and deal with these behaviors property. Early intervention works, and companies need to develop strategies to deal with issues before crises develop.

After treatment I was fortunate to have a second chance to build a career again in the business world. When I returned to working life, I decided not to keep my recovery a secret. I let people know my story, and I was surprised to find out many people had friends, family members, and associates who were struggling with addictions. The more I talked to people, the more they opened up and shared their concerns, feelings, and fears, as well as their frustrations, on not knowing what to do with addictions in their homes and offices. This gave me a business idea.

In many ways I was much more successful in business after treatment than I ever was before—but there was something

"A few of us are getting together after work to binge-drink. You're welcome to join us if you're not in recovery."

"A few of us are getting together after work to binge-drink. You're welcome to join us if you're not in recovery." Cartoon by Mike Baldwin. www.CartoonStock.com.

missing. I had lost interest in selling products and services that really didn't make a difference to people. I was motivated to help people, and I believed there was a way to do that and build a business, as well. I left comfortable corporate America and took a leap of faith.

My new company, Addiction Intervention Resources, Inc., has made a lot of progress raising the issue of addiction in business and educating others, but we have a lot of work to do. Many corporations are still in the dark with regard to addictions in the workplace. Denial is a huge factor. Many use the strategy of "don't ask, don't tell," and if there is a problem, executives don't want to know about it unless there is a drug- or alcohol-related accident or someone shows up to work drunk or high.

Sure, companies pay for EAP services, and insurance may cover treatment, but these services require the addicted individual to self-report and ask for help. This by itself is a failed approach, because most people who use drugs in the workplace are either in denial or too afraid to ask for help, fearing reprisal. Shame is a huge factor, and most addicted individuals are just not going to walk in and ask for help.

Businesses have an obligation to step in and be more aggressive in addressing addictions in the workplace by intervening more proactively. Businesses need to face the problem head-on before it gets to the point where the organization is negatively affected. What it boils down to is corporate culture and doing what's right for the company, employees, customers, and stockholders.

Companies can take seven steps to deal with these issues, and EAPs would be wise to share them with their clients:

1. Educate the workforce about addiction and treatment.

2. Promote company-wide use of EAPs.

3. Create a proactive addiction workplace policy.

4. When prevention and policy fail, intervene early.

5. Invest in healthcare that provides coverage for treatment.

6. Support employees in recovery and reentry into the workplace.

7. Maintain a healthy corporate culture.

On the Other End

It's not easy to intervene. It's contrary to the actions we like to take. Believe me, I've experienced it firsthand.

Most of the employees at Addiction Intervention Resources are recovering alcoholics and addicts. Recently, one of them relapsed and started using drugs again. Although I knew her history, and my business is about advising clients on these issues, as her boss it was difficult to confront her. Two factors made it difficult for me. First, I didn't want to go through the process of having to confront her and deal with it. The second was from a purely business perspective: Despite being addicted, she did a good job and was an important employee; I didn't want to lose her and the work she did. I was almost willing to put up with the addiction.

This situation put the problem into perspective for me and clearly showed me what others in business are faced with every day. We eventually did take action, and she is currently in treatment. We've developed a return-to-work strategy for her and will support her recovery, but we will not enable her to use again without consequences at work.

I don't know how this will turn out for her and our company, but at least we took action. We were not part of the conspiracy of silence in the workplace; we confronted and helped her, which is ultimately good business policy. Maybe we helped to save her life, too—the ultimate bottom-line decision.

Many people believe that alcoholics and drug users are just homeless people living under bridges and on the streets. However, according to SAMHSA more than 75% of illicit drug users are employed either full or part time, and more than 80% of the 43 million adult binge drinkers and 12.4 million heavy drinkers are employed. According to a Hazelden Foundation addiction in the workplace survey, nearly 60% of adults know someone who has reported for work under the influence of alcohol or other drugs; it's obvious this is a problem that needs to be addressed.

What it all comes down to is that addiction in the workplace costs businesses billions of dollars every year. Treatment works, and early intervention is simply *the best* way to motivate someone who is unable or unwilling to ask for help.

| *"It is often the family member who provides . . . the 'grace moment' that can bring success to an otherwise difficult intervention."*

Family and Friends Play Important Roles in Interventions

Nancy Doyle Palmer

Nancy Doyle Palmer is a writer for the Washingtonian. *In this viewpoint, she describes the process of intervention for alcoholism and drug addiction, and the important role families and friends can play in moving an addict toward treatment. She contends that the role of family members in getting an addict to treatment is crucial.*

As you read, consider the following questions:

1. Who are some of the celebrities named by Palmer who have had to decide about participating in an intervention?
2. Why do some interventionists believe they have to "create the crisis" in order to get an addict into treatment, according to the author?

3. What does Palmer say about the possibility of relapses and the likelihood that an intervention will be successful?

*I*t was a Saturday morning, and I was in the basement of my house in Mount Vernon [Virginia] asleep on the couch with half-gallon bottles of alcohol underneath the cushions. My wife came down and told me there were people upstairs who wanted to talk to me.

Ted's Story

I came upstairs into the living room, and she sat down and joined my eldest son home from college, my second son home from college, my daughter, two of my partners and one of my associates from the law firm, and a counselor named Susan. They started talking, and I can't remember any of what they said because I was in such a fog, but I do recall that there was no preaching, no badmouthing, no threats, just tears and concern that I was killing myself. They all said something, and when they got to Susan, she said, "We think we need to get you to the hospital." And I looked out, and they had all lined up their cars along the driveway, and my first thought was how am I going to get in my car and get the hell out of there. But my second thought was I knew I couldn't do that—there were a lot of important people in the room, and I'll have to go along with this.

It's called an intervention—family, friends, coworkers, even the boss surprise and confront an addict and insist on immediate treatment.

[Former first lady] Betty Ford is glad she had one, and [former US senator] George McGovern wished he'd done one. Apparently [former president] George W. Bush didn't need one.

Betty Ford's intervention was orchestrated by her family and facilitated by the founding father of interventions, Vernon Johnson, in 1978. It became the stuff of legend in the recovery movement and led to the former first lady's creation of the Betty Ford Center in California.

George McGovern laments in a foreword to *Love First*, the guidebook of the pioneering Hazelden addiction-treatment organization, that his family resisted confronting their alcoholic daughter. "We were repeatedly told by well-meaning, supposedly informed friends that we would have to wait until Terry really 'hit bottom.' The trouble is that when she hit bottom, she died." Terry McGovern froze to death on the streets of Madison, Wisconsin, one December night in 1994.

While Washington [DC] is no stranger to addiction and the attendant stories of falls from grace and redemption, the city has a more complicated relationship with interventions, although one takes place almost every day here. But taking the step to organize friends, family, and coworkers to confront an addict isn't easy.

Babette Wise, director of the Alcohol and Drug Abuse Program at Georgetown University Hospital, calls the problem the "sea of silence and secrets."

Love First co-author and interventionist Jeff Jay has spent a lot of time in Washington and agrees it's a tough town. "These people are going to be much more worried about the stigma of chemical dependency than most people," he says. "DC is a brutally competitive town, and many of these people got to the position they are in by being control freaks, so they tend to be uncompromising in negotiations they aren't in favor of."

Washington Is Different

Bob Poznanovich and Andrew Wainwright are founders of Addiction Intervention Resources, a national organization based in Minneapolis. They say Washington is different. "The ultra rich and the ultra powerful are typically the ones who don't contact us," says Poznanovich. "They don't reach the same level of pain as other families do, and they often have people around them to fix things."

Wainwright grew up in DC, went to St. Albans and Gonzaga, and studied at Georgetown and Catholic Universities before his own drug-and-alcohol abuse landed him in rehab 11 years ago.

"I love Washington, but it's a hard town," he says. "There's not a lot of tolerance for weakness. My mother finally stopped caring what other people thought. She had me admitted to a locked ward at a hospital and intervened on me there. I agreed to go to treatment and went with them to the airport. But I still thought I was in control. When I found out it was a one-way ticket to Hazelden, I went nuts and slugged my mom! With the help of the intervention team they got me onto the plane to Minnesota. I actually hit my mother—I wasn't raised to do that, but that's where my disease took me."

His organization advocates lengthy preparation and bringing as much leverage as possible into an intervention. "You bring a gun to a gunfight, not a knife," he says. "Especially in DC—it's a power town, and this is a power disease. We want to give the power back to the family, to the wife and kids who have been walking on eggshells, where the disease runs the entire show, where a good day or a bad day is dictated by the disease."

The primary tenet of intervention is that it's not a good idea to wait for the addict to "hit bottom." Wainwright's partner, Poznanovich, says, "If you had a growth on the side of your neck and it was getting bigger and bigger, your family wouldn't buy you a scarf; they would take you to the best cancer facility in the world, whether you wanted them to or not." Addiction is "the big elephant in the room," he says. "You can't pretend it's not there."

A Revolutionary Approach

Although the self-described "young Turks" Wainwright and Poznanovich say they are the vanguard of the new world of intervention with a variety of services, they credit Vernon Johnson with creating the original model that works to this day.

In the early 1960s, Johnson came to the revolutionary conclusion that alcoholism and drug abuse were delusional diseases that prevented the addict from seeking help. This helped dispel the idea that an alcoholic or addict must be ready for help before he or she can be helped. Rather than wait for the alcoholic to bottom out, a group of caring people could "create the crisis" and motivate the addict to accept treatment.

The traditional model for interventions stresses that it is neither an emotional ambush nor an uncaring attack but rather a carefully prepared, structured confrontation that leaves the addict with no choice than to change.

Often with the help of a professional interventionist, a group of people close to the addict—spouse, parents, siblings, children, friends, coworkers—come together to confront the addict with prepared statements or letters to be read aloud.

The message to the addict is threefold; how much the addict means to the person, how specific behavior resulting from the addiction has damaged that relationship, and what changes will now take place in the relationship unless the addict seeks help. One expert calls this "presenting an authentic mirror of behavior and harm done" and establishes a leverage that gives the addict no choice but to accept the help being offered.

Leverage can be as minor as refusing to spend time with the addict or as major as divorce or getting fired. The element of surprise is crucial. Despite the apprehension that the subject will just get up and walk out, that happens rarely. Another fear is that any treatment that is coerced will be unsuccessful. Statistics show that once an addict goes into treatment, the chances of recovery are exactly the same as for those who accept treatment without an intervention.

Elizabeth's Story

The first intervention we did for my mother failed. It was professionally done, with my two brothers and sister there, my father and grandmother, and my mother's best friend. After she checked in, we all left town, and my mother was home from the center two days later and drunk again.

Another 20 years went by, basically just getting by until last year, when she stopped eating. So we tried it again. We got ten people together, including my brothers and eight women friends of hers in their sixties and seventies—the women who had taught with her, written with her, traveled with her, and had watched her deteriorate.

They told her she had embarrassed herself and was no good professionally anymore. We told her she had no relationship with her grandchildren, we couldn't come to her with any problems, and she was poisoning herself.

None of it got through to her. She was defiant, mad, thanked us for coming, and told us to leave. So my brother and I took her into another room, and I kneeled down next to her wheelchair and took her hand and said, "I'm sorry but if one of my kids had a serious disease, I would just pick them up and take them. And whether you like this or not, that's what we're doing." And we each put a hand under her arm and started to lift her up.

She said "You can't do this to me," but the minute she was up-right she said, "I guess I'll need my purse."

Vaughn Howland, founder and director of the Intervention Center, has been conducting interventions in the Washington area for more than 20 years. He likens his work to "staging a play." His signature style is conducting interventions with formality and respect. "If you prepare yourself, then everyone knows what they are going to do and not do, read their script, and shut up," he says. "Everyone does their thing, and the person just sits there and sweats."

He adds that while he is very concerned about the addict, "My primary focus is the family. I want the family to get through this no matter what happens. I want them to be able to say, 'No matter what happens, we gave it our best shot.'"

Jeff Jay says that he sometimes has to fine-tune interventions in Washington. "Sometimes the addict knows there is something in the offing, and I go in and talk one-on-one first. They like me for calling it off—it puts them in their executive-thinking mode, and they listen to me." He adds that he often gives over small points of control to the addict in negotiating treatment. "I once allowed one person in the course of the intervention to change

Family Intervention Can Start the Healing

When an addicted person is reluctant to seek help, sometimes family members, friends, and associates come together out of concern and love, to confront the problem drinker. They strongly urge the person to enter treatment and list the serious consequences of not doing so, such as family breakup or job loss.

This is called "intervention."

Substance Abuse and Mental Health Services Administration, September 2005. http://store.samhsa.gov.

where he was going for treatment from one side of the country to another. This made him feel empowered."

Families Can Feel Relieved

Even if the subject refuses treatment or accepts help only to relapse later, the families often feel a sense of catharsis and relief at getting the secret out. Ground rules have been established, patterns of enabling or hiding the addiction have been broken.

"My father died five months after an intervention for Valium abuse that led to a disastrous stay in rehab," says a Washington reporter, "but my conscience is clear. We did everything we could to stop him."

Beth Kane Davidson, director of Suburban Hospital's Addiction Treatment Center, emphasizes the delicacy of the process. "Intervention is an art," she says. "It's not just 'Okay, we'll get a person in and tell them the bad things they've done and that they need treatment.' You're talking about a technique, a process.

"It's not true that you can't help somebody until they want help," she says. "You can raise the bottom."

Davidson says interventions that don't work are usually the result of a weak link in the group, someone who threatens but does not follow through and continues to enable. The toughest interventions? "When it comes out that the spouse is a drinker as well."

But it is often the family member who provides what Georgetown University's Babette Wise calls the "grace moment" that can bring success to an otherwise difficult intervention. "One of the first ones I ever did involved a grandfather with his adult children and grandchildren," she recalls. "A seven-year-old little girl said to him, 'I'm not going to get in a car with you. I don't have fun with you anymore. I'm not going to play with you anymore.'"

Howland agrees. "I love to have children there—there is nothing like having a little girl with ribbons in her hair and tears streaming down her face," he says. . . .

Only the First Step

Most addiction experts stress that an intervention is just one step in what is often a very long haul.

"An awful lot of people put their emotional eggs in the basket of what will happen on intervention day," says Intervention Center founder Vaughn Howland. "It's just a kickoff point no matter how they do—it's a three-to-five-year process in the best of circumstances."

Ginna Marston, of the Partnership for a Drug-Free America, agrees: "Intervention as a one-hit thing is going to disappoint."

Recovery, whether it's the classic 28-day inpatient stay at a rehabilitation facility or outpatient treatments like AA [Alcoholics Anonymous], is not immediate, not easy, and not always successful. Relapses are common, and families often have to be prepared for bigger changes than just sobriety, such as divorce, estrangement from children or friends, even career changes.

"Intervention carries with it the possibility of change," says Marston. "Change that may be better for the addict, but for some of those people in the old comfort zone, the change can be threatening and frightening."

Many area interventions conclude with a packed bag and a short car trip to Father Martin's Ashley, a highly regarded treatment facility in southern Maryland. "The bottom line is whatever works," says program director Christopher Shea. "What I've learned from my years in the field is that it doesn't matter to me what gets someone into treatment, whether someone feels tricked into this or is only here because of someone else. You're here for 28 days, and what are you going to do with that?

"You can go kicking and screaming into treatment, but it may save your life."

Of the more than 22 million people in America dealing with addiction, 19 million are not getting or seeking help. Most experts call for any kind of intervention as soon and as often as possible. "My fantasy is that one day it's handled like heart disease or cancer," says Babette Wise, "where the doctor sees someone who is alcoholic and says, 'Next time bring in a family member,' like in any other potential life-threatening diagnosis, and address it directly. A mini intervention could happen in the emergency room—where at least 25 percent of the visits from falls or car accidents are alcohol-related."

One of the area's leading recovery advocacy organizations is the Johnson Institute—named after the intervention pioneer Vernon Johnson. President Johnny Allem says that there is much to hope for. "The briefest of interventions, just 15 minutes with a doctor or a pastor, can have tremendous impact," he says.

He adds that although cutbacks in insurance coverage by managed care have created barriers to treatment, "the effectiveness of early intervention has been thoroughly documented, including practices of very short duration by professionals who witness early symptoms of addiction disease." These professional practices have been called "brief interventions" and are endorsed by the American Society of Addiction Medicine.

"This is not costly," he adds. "Financing early treatment and recovery drives down primary healthcare costs. And doing the right thing pays for itself. It just takes the courage to overcome discrimination and the myths surrounding alcohol-and-drug addiction."

A member of another DC-based group, Faces and Voices of Recovery, worries that George W. Bush's solo effort to quit drinking sent the wrong message to those who think they can handle their addictions without help: "George Bush comes to town, and the impression they try to convey is that he just suddenly realized he had a problem and he stopped drinking and lived happily ever after."

And if an intervention fails? "There's no such thing," says Suburban's Beth Kane. "You've planted a seed. So many come back a year, even two years, later and say, 'Everything you say is true.' It's not a failure, because you've put it out on the table."

And you can always try again.

> *"It is highly recommended that you get involved in AL-ANON, CODA (co-dependency), or any other 12-step group supporting the family and significant others of loved ones who are addicted."*

Families Involved in Interventions Should Seek Help and Support

Gerard "Jerry" J. Egan

Gerard J. Egan is a social worker and the program director for Palm Partners Recovery Center in West Palm Beach, Florida. In this viewpoint he describes the stress, fear, anxiety, and disappointment that can be experienced by an addict's family members and recommends strategies for self-care, including seeking help and support from others.

As you read, consider the following questions:

1. In what ways does the author say that addiction harms relationships?

Gerard "Jerry" J. Egan and Thomas Beley, "Twisted Relationships: Recovery Wreckage," AlcoholicsAnonymous.com, July 28, 2010. Copyright © 2010 by Gerard J. Egan and Thomas Beley. All rights reserved. Reproduced by permission.

2. What are some of the organizations Egan suggests family members can turn to for help in dealing with addiction?

3. Why, in the author's opinion, is it important for an addict's family members to be able to say no?

B eing involved in the addictions treatment business for over thirty years I have witnessed the damage and trauma that substance use, abuse and dependency have inflicted on families and friends of an addict or alcoholic. Most of the time the impact is clearly experienced but rarely ever fully understood. It is my hope today to clarify the severe misunderstandings that occur to the family and their relationship with the addict or alcoholic. It is my opinion that many times a person will relapse due to the confusion and frustration they experience when dealing with the significant others in their lives. In fact relationship problems are probably the number one reason that a recovering person will fail to recover.

To begin our discussion it is first necessary to outline in as simple a manner as possible the reasons that any human being searches for and develops a relationship. Relationships by their definition are designed to allow people to get their needs met. Whenever people approach each other it is for the purpose of needs satisfaction; otherwise there would be no reason for the contact. This is the same whether it is a simple transaction with a cashier at the food store or a deep emotional exchange between two lovers; the reason for the interaction is for the satisfaction of human needs.

Addiction poisons the interaction between people in the following manner: It causes many powerful and negative feelings and emotions that interfere with the ability to get needs met. Due to living with the addict or alcoholic the person has experienced confusion, despair, betrayal, deceit, disillusionment, anxiety, fear, worry, anger, frustration, desperation, depression, terror, sadness—and this is just a very short list of the emotional impacts. The result of this emotional damage is that the significant other becomes very hesitant in their willingness or ability to help meet the emotional and intimacy needs of the addict or alcoholic. It is this hesitation that the addict experiences as rejection and that triggers relapse. Since their significant other has rejected them, or they just simply do not have the ability to meet those needs, the addict then runs for the cover and comfort that substances provide.

When an addict or alcoholic relapses numerous times the family becomes very hesitant to believe in that person. Anytime someone believes in someone they are manifesting much hope that things can change and improve. When a person relapses after their family or significant other had built up hope; the pain of losing hope causes such intense suffering that the person becomes very reluctant in becoming enthusiastic or excited about the addict's latest recovery attempts. They develop a "fear of having hope." It is only by risking having hope that they can be hurt again; and by being negative or even cynical towards the belief that the person can and will recover, they in fact are protecting themselves from emotional pain and suffering. The addict and alcoholic view their reluctance to show any enthusiasm or encouragement as rejection and the pain of rejection can certainly cause the loss of recovery.

The addict must recognize that all people have a right to protect themselves from injury and the addict must not take it personally if their significant other is reluctant or hesitant in demonstrating support and enthusiasm while they are in early recovery. The family or significant other is simply taking a wait-and-see attitude. It is in this manner that they protect themselves from disappointment. If they do not show or feel hope then they cannot suffer the great pain associated with having their hope taken away when the person relapses. Therefore it is helpful for the addict to accept that their significant other is not trying to hurt them but is just trying to protect themselves from having their hope destroyed one more time.

Get Involved

Not in your loved one's recovery, but in your own. You need to remember that you are in a process of recovery yourself. The only difference between your loved one's recovery and yours is that in many instances you have felt the pain and misery every step of the way. You have witnessed the suffering and have felt the pain of that suffering. Your loved one was often intoxicated or too high to notice the pain they were creating. Although they are very much aware of the pain at this moment that their abusing and using has caused, you have been aware of this pain and misery for awhile now. To that end, it is important to take care of yourself. To do that it is highly recommended that you get involved in AL-ANON, CODA (co-dependency), or any other 12-step group supporting the family and significant others of loved ones who are addicted. These self-help groups are usually readily accessible throughout your community offering the necessary support, help, and guidance in, not only better understanding the disease concept of addiction, but in better understanding what it is that you need to do to take care of yourself and your loved one. These support groups are made up of those who have walked or are walking in the same path as yourself. These groups can offer you the necessary support, guidance, and help in making decisions about what is best for you and your loved one's future. Chances are that you will still need to make some very difficult decisions about your loved one in the future, it is best that you don't do it alone but with the help of those who have been through this before.

If you are finding it difficult to attend these groups, you may want to consider therapy or family therapy. It is not uncommon for the family to have endured long periods of stress, fear, tension, and anxiety. In some instances, the family and significant others have been traumatized by the behaviors of the addicted loved one. Depression, anxiety, and stress disorders for the family are all too often common fallout of the addictive process. Just because your loved one may have made the decision to get involved in treatment it doesn't mean that your stress and anxiety is about to leave you. Research has shown that stress and tension remains within the physiological makeup of a person for extended periods of time. In certain instances, this stress and tension can actually remain within the body leading not only to emotional difficulties but also contributing to physical illnesses. Sitting down with a trained therapist who is knowledgeable in the field of addictions and recovery can offer extremely useful insight into the recovery process. Therapy isn't as time consuming as it once was and someone who is specifically trained in the field of addictions can be extremely useful. Professionals trained in the field of addictions are very much aware of the difficulties that you have been through and know precisely many of the issues you may be struggling with.

Another good way you can become involved is by reading the Alcoholics Anonymous "Big Book." The principles, or the 12 steps, that are outlined in the book have been a mainstay and foundation of the recovery movement since its inception in 1939. Alcoholics Anonymous is located throughout the world and has helped and is helping tens of millions of people on a daily basis suffering from addiction. The reason that Alcoholics Anonymous has been credited with being so effective over the years is believed to be in part due to the result of people adhering to the principles of the 12 steps. One of the arguments that we often hear is that the "Big Book" is a religious oriented book and that the book focuses on God too much. Nothing can be further from the truth. Although the "Big Book" does focus on the concept of a God, it focuses more on the perspective of a higher power and the importance of a person achieving a spiritual awakening. The 12 steps are nothing more than simple basic principles on how to live life. The philosophy behind these principles is that by following and working these steps a spiritual awakening will occur allowing us to live a more peaceful, content, and prosperous lifestyle. As we often point out to the people we work with, most successful people, not just those suffering from an addictive disorder, follow the 12 steps. They just don't know that they are following the principles of Alcoholics Anonymous. One would be hard pressed not to see the beauty and simplicity of these basic principles. . . . Please take a look at them and by all means take a closer look at the "Big Book" to see how they are integrated into a person's recovery.

Just Say No

One of the more important steps that the family and significant others can take in their loved one's recovery is to learn to say "NO!" As you are probably all too aware, this word is easier to think about than it is to actually say. But it is absolutely crucial that you learn how to say it and your loved one learns how to hear it. And when you say "no," it is important to say "no" to everything. Regardless of how minor or reasonable the request may seem you need to simply say "No!" This is not to teach your loved one a lesson about his or her past choices or to help you practice "tough love." Saying "no" and learning to hear "no" is an extremely important step in changing behavior patterns. Changing the behavior patterns of individuals is one of the most important elements to a successful recovery.

Who was it that your loved one called in times of a crisis? Who was called at the last moment to solve a problem? There is no secret here. In a majority of instances, it was you. Saying "no" sets in motion a new way of thinking and, more importantly, a new set of behaviors. One of the behaviors that your loved one needs to accomplish is for your loved one to think through their particular dilemma, no matter how small, and to tap into their own problem-solving potential and capabilities. All too often people suffering from an addictive disorder have a tendency to look for the "short cut" to a problem or want that instant gratification. All too often, that "shortcut" has been you. By simply saying "no," even to the smallest request, forces your loved one to start thinking and behaving differently. Even more importantly, it places the person in a position of problem-solving. This is ex-

Families Should Seek Help When Dealing with Addicts

There is a reason that families find it necessary to hire a skilled interventionist to conduct an intervention—to raise the bottom for their loved one so that they can see how their addiction is affecting everyone in their life. . . . No one expects a family to instinctually know how to appropriately care for a loved one with an addiction, but there are resources out there to help with this process.

Psychology Today, *April 12, 2011.*

actly what needs to be accomplished. By doing this, the person has an opportunity to tap into or develop appropriate problem-solving skills by thinking about their particular dilemma and all the possible ways it can be solved. Up to this point in time, they have usually depended on only two sources for their solutions: you or the substance. When the family or significant relationship is not readily accessible as a "shortcut," they are more prone to ask their peers, staff, or therapist regarding a solution. This is what allows your loved one to begin to develop or tap into their problem-solving skills. Another important facet of this process is getting the person to build up their frustration tolerance rather than getting immediate gratification.

Be Prepared

Now that you understand the rationale behind the "no" and are hopefully practicing it, guess what happens next? Anger, and a lot of it. It is usually directed at others but you will get your fair share too. In the beginning, most of the complaints will be directed to what went wrong in your loved one's life and what is going wrong now. Your loved one is sure that we don't understand their situation and that we lack the necessary compassion and caring that it is going to take in order for them to get better. Well, nothing is further from the truth and the best way to understand this process is to think in term of "green beans and ice cream."

The brain in the early part of recovery is not too different than a very hungry 10 year old child who hasn't eaten all day long. Think about it. Imagine a 10 year old that hasn't eaten all day long. They come home and are being offered a choice between a big bowl of green beans and a big bowl of ice cream to satisfy their hunger. I wonder which one they are going to choose.

Your loved one has been consuming massive amounts of "ice cream" for months and in many instances years in order to satisfy their hunger. There is no way they are going to choose the "green beans" over the "ice cream." This is usually the time that your loved one will be experiencing their most frustration and anger. Your loved one will be convinced that this is not the place for them to recover and "get me out of here or else" is likely to be their rallying cry for you to give in to their threats, demands, and promises. Do not give in. This phase is typically short-lived and temporary. You have to remember that their discomfort and pain in the early part of treatment is for the most part [rooted in their] not getting their way.

Probably one of the most influential forces that a person can have in their recovery is their family or significant other support system. Not that it is the responsibility of the family to get their loved one to recover, but the family can be an extremely helpful support in reminding their loved one about the process of recovery. Often time recovery is not a steady state of progression. Rather, it is a process of two steps forward and one step back. By following some of these basic guidelines regarding a loved one's recovery, the family can be an enormous on-going support.

| "It is hoped that screening, intervention and referral will become standard medical care."

Doctors Should Be Trained to Intervene During Routine Medical Care

Larry M. Gentilello

Larry M. Gentilello is a professor of surgery at the University of Texas Southwestern Medical Center in Dallas. In this viewpoint he argues that screening for alcohol and substance abuse, followed by brief intervention when needed, should be a routine part of providing health care for all medical specialties and in many health care settings, because of its proven effectiveness.

As you read, consider the following questions:

1. What does SBIRT stand for, as used by the author?
2. Why does the author claim that interventions that take place in hospital trauma centers have a high rate of success?
3. How will health care reform impact the ability of patients to get treatment for addiction and substance abuse problems, according to Gentilello?

It wasn't too long ago that addiction treatment specialists were the only source of professional help to those suffering from problems with alcohol and drugs. But in recent years, screening, brief intervention and referral to treatment (SBIRT) of patients with potential alcohol- and drug-related problems has increasingly become a part of mainstream medicine.

First introduced in the late 1990s, SBIRT addresses the entire spectrum of substance use disorders, from early symptoms that are identified and addressed before the patient has exhibited signs of addiction to addicted patients who need long-term chronic treatment. The approach is evidence-based, and has demonstrated a small but proven impact on daily and weekly alcohol consumption, DUI arrests, injuries, car crashes and other complications associated with alcohol and drug misuse.

Now, physicians and healthcare providers of all stripes (those in trauma centers, emergency departments, primary care and college campus health clinics, general surgical and medical wards, and employee assistance programs) increasingly are using formal screening methods to detect the potential harmful use of alcohol, prescription drugs, or illicit drugs. And physicians and other hospital and clinic staff are also counseling patients who screen positive for substance use and are referring some on for treatment by addiction specialists.

There is a great deal of other evidence that the momentum for the SBIRT approach continues to grow:

- A new medical specialty board, the American Board of Addiction Medicine, was established in 2007 and already has certified nearly 3,000 physicians from various disciplines as specialists in addiction medicine.

- Medicare, and in some states Medicaid, is reimbursing clinicians for these services. New CPT [current procedural terminology] codes for reimbursing brief intervention activities were adopted. Effective in January 2007, the Centers for Medicare & Medicaid Services (CMS) allowed reimbursement for alcohol- and drug-related screening and brief interventions.

• Barriers to SBIRT are falling. For instance, many states have repealed insurance laws that discourage blood alcohol test screening in emergency departments. A widely adopted state insurance law recommended in 1947 by the National Association of Insurance Commissioners (NAIC) allowed health insurance companies to deny payment to physicians and healthcare providers for medical care to persons injured as a result of being under the influence of alcohol or a non-prescribed narcotic. As a result of these laws, one in four trauma surgeons were experiencing denials of reimbursement and only half of trauma surgeons surveyed were screening patients for blood alcohol content. Fortunately, progress has been made in repealing these laws. In 2001, the NAIC unanimously recommended that states repeal the laws, and since then 14 states and the District of Columbia have done so.

The leading question now for "traditional" addiction treatment professionals is how much this trend will affect public health and their livelihoods. Will there be fewer referrals to addiction treatment specialists? Will these specialty providers have to compete with doctors for patients? Or will they receive more referrals and develop closer ties and stronger relationships with physicians?

Those are legitimate questions, but first it might be helpful to place this trend into some historical perspective.

What's Behind the SBIRT Trend?

The mainstreaming of SBIRT reflects a growing acknowledgement that alcohol and drug use can endanger the health of people who do not have, by definition, an addiction.

Although alcohol and other drugs cause or complicate the treatment of at least 70 medical conditions for which patients frequently seek care, medical schools and residency training programs traditionally have provided very little practical training for doctors on how to screen for substance use and intervene when necessary.

As a result, in any given year, 22 million Americans are in need of substance use treatment, yet only two million patients each year receive it. Why is that? The main reason is 94 percent of patients simply don't know they need treatment. Four percent know they need treatment but don't want it, and two percent know they need help and are actively seeking it or wanting to engage in it.

When it comes to addressing alcohol or drug use problems, one of the most important developments in the past 20 years has been the recognition that only a relatively small fraction of the patients who use alcohol or drugs in quantities that can damage their health meet the criteria for having alcohol dependence syndrome or alcoholism, or are drug addicts.

This was shown by the largest study on SBIRT, a 2009 analysis that screened 459,599 patients in general medical settings (including emergency departments, family practice clinics, trauma centers and general medical surgical wards).

The study found that 22.7 percent of patients had a positive screen for some type of alcohol or drug problem. The two most commonly identified problems were binge drinking (getting drunk to the point of intoxication) and regular use of alcohol in amounts that might not lead to intoxication, but that over time can cause chronic health problems. These two types of drinking patterns were found in 15.9 percent of patients. However, the severity of the problem was at a level that most patients were judged to need only one skillfully delivered counseling session.

The study found that an additional 3.2 percent of patients had problems that were more advanced but still did not meet the definition of addiction or dependence. However, it was felt that these individuals would benefit from more than one counseling session, and should be seen at least two or three more times. The patient's primary physician, regardless of specialty, can provide these sessions if he/she receives the proper training.

The SBIRT trial found that only 3.7 percent of patients who present for general medical care—about one in six of those who screened positive—met the definition of addiction, or suffered from the alcohol dependence syndrome. These patients need to be referred to an outpatient or inpatient center for treatment by an addiction treatment specialist or someone with similar professional credentials.

Proven Value in Trauma

What addiction professionals have learned is that "the setting" often plays an important role in the effectiveness of the screening and brief intervention. SBIRT has proven to be especially valuable in trauma centers, because nearly 50 percent of the time, alcohol or drugs played a key role in the event that led to the patient's injuries. SBIRT appears to be particularly effective in trauma centers.

One study showed that a year after a trauma center intervention, patients reduced their alcohol consumption by an average of nearly 22 drinks per week (a control group that did not have an intervention reduced their drinking by only six drinks per week).[1] Over the following year there was a 48 percent reduction in return visits to an ER for treatment of another major or minor injury. There was still a benefit three years later, as the intervention group had a 47 percent reduction in injuries that were serious enough to require readmission to the hospital.[1]

Another study showed that by reducing the risk of reinjury, each time it provides an intervention it saves $330 in healthcare costs over the next three years. The return on investment was $3.81 saved for every $1 spent on screening and intervention.[2]

The role that SBIRT could play in transforming healthcare was underscored when the American College of Surgeons Committee on Trauma (COT), the primary organization responsible for

The SBIRT Model

The beauty of the Screening, Brief Intervention, and Referral to Treatment model (SBIRT) is that it is simple, brief, and can be integrated into regular check-ups or interviews to initially detect and subsequently monitor changes in substance use. The model can be used in a variety of settings from health to social service and education. Built on a solid base of research, science-based demonstration projects have proven so successful that SAMHSA CSAT [Substance Abuse and Mental Health Services Administration, Center for Substance Abuse Treatment] Director, Dr. H. Westley Clark has announced that "promoting services like SBIRT . . . is a crucial part of SAMHSA's mission to reach everyone struggling with substance abuse issues" (SAMHSA News, 2009).

Addiction Technology Transfer Center
Network, Addiction Messenger, *July 2010.*
www.nattc.org.

developing trauma center requirements, added a new criterion for Level 1 trauma center verification. Starting in the spring of 2007 the COT required all Level 1 trauma centers to have a mechanism to screen for substance use problems for all patients who sustained injuries serious enough to require admission to the trauma center. And all Level 1 trauma centers had to have a mechanism in place to provide an intervention to those who screened positive.

The American College of Surgeons was the first professional medical society that had regulatory authority to pass a requirement that patients receive treatment for a substance use problem. For that matter, it became the first medical society that mandated any type of mental health benefit for patients receiving medical care.[3]

Prior to this mandate, screening for alcohol problems in trauma centers was far from routine.[4] A 1999 study based on a random sampling of 241 members of the American Association for the Surgery of Trauma reported that more than half of trauma surgeons screened fewer than one in four of their patients.[5]

Given the rarity of screening, and lack of interventions and referrals prior to the new COT ruling, it is anticipated that the currently required use of SBIRT in trauma centers will increase the number of patients screened. More patients who require the services of addiction treatment professionals will be identified, and referred. However, the big payoff will come when the practice of screening and interventions spreads from trauma centers, and begins to involve hospital settings in general.

The trauma center mandate for use of screening and brief intervention has ignited the fuse that we hope will eventually lead to the spread of screening, intervention and referral to specialty care for those who need it, to many other types of general medical practices.

What It Means for the Addiction Professional

Now that SBIRT has been adopted in trauma centers, it is hoped that screening, intervention and referral will become standard medical care. Studies have shown that SBIRT is one of the most beneficial and cost-effective preventive healthcare measures available (more than screening for cholesterol, cervical cancer, diabetes and depression—preventive measures that already *are* standard medical practices in many settings).

There are reasons to believe that the trend to adopt SBIRT will accelerate. More and more doctors are becoming board-certified in addiction medicine; hospitals are increasingly developing expertise in performing SBIRT; and young, new physicians are beginning to accept that addressing substance use problems is a part of their core responsibilities.

There has never been a better opportunity to break down the barriers between mainstream medicine and substance use treatment, and to make sure patients with problematic alcohol or drug use are identified and get the help they need. After all, healthcare reform will now require most Americans to have health insurance coverage, and the new federal Mental Health Parity and Addiction Equity Act will increase accessibility to insurance average for treatment of addiction and mental health problems.

The bottom line is that SBIRT is a welcome addition in the fight against dangerous use of alcohol and other drugs. It has the potential to alert an increasing portion of the more than 20 million people who may have a potential problem and need to seek help. And while patients with mild problems will receive counseling from their doctor, those with complicated or severe problems will be referred to addiction treatment specialists.

As screening becomes routine in general medical care, physicians who identify patients in need of more than brief intervention or counseling will have to have arrangements with addiction treatment specialists who possess the skills and who work at facilities that can provide the more extensive treatment and ongoing care that these patients require.

As adoption of SBIRT into medical care increases, early identification and intervention might result in fewer patients developing the need to be seen by an addiction treatment professional. On the other hand, 90 percent of patients who require help don't even know it. The adoption of SBIRT in healthcare settings will identify these patients and result in *more*, not fewer, patients being referred for the type of addiction treatment that most general medical doctors cannot provide. Society will need *more* addiction professionals, not fewer. Ultimately, that's good not only for patients, but also for society at large—and for those who treat them.

Notes

1. Gentilello LM, Rivara FP, Donovan DM et al. Alcohol interventions in a trauma center as a means of reducing the risk of injury recurrence. Ann Surg 1999 Oct;230:473–80.

2. Gentilello LM, Ebel BE, Wickizer TM et al. Alcohol interventions for trauma patients treated in emergency departments and hospitals: a cost benefit anlysis. Ann Surg 2005 Apr;241:541–50.

3. Mello MJ. Rhode Island Hospital Injury Prevention Center Translation of Alcohol Screening and Brief Intervention Guidelines to Pediatric Trauma Centers, grant from Injury Control Research Centers. www.cdc.gov/injury/erpo/Funding/ICRC2009.html.

4. Terrell F, Zatzick DF, Junkovich GJ et al. Nationwide survey of alcohol screening and brief intervention practices at US Level I trauma centers. J Am Coll Surg 2008 Nov;207:630–8.

5. Danielsson PE. Reasons why trauma surgeons fail to screen for alcohol problems. Arch Surg 1999 May;134:564–8.

Periodical and Internet Sources Bibliography

The following articles have been selected to supplement the diverse views presented in this chapter.

Amy Brown-Bowers	"Functioning Addicts," *Globe and Mail* (Toronto), March 31, 2009.
Rebecca A. Clay	"Screening, Brief Intervention, and Referral to Treatment: New Populations, New Effectiveness Data," *SAMHSA News*, November/December, 2009.
Marcus Hersch	"Michael Baze's Death a Wake-Up Call for Racing," *Daily Racing Form*, June 30, 2011.
Eamon Keane	"Our Love of Booze Is Out of Control," *Irish Independent* (Dublin), April 27, 2008.
Marketwire	"Drug and Alcohol Rehab Costs a Fraction of the Cost of Addiction: A Successful Drug and Alcohol Rehab Program Could Save Billions for U.S. Taxpayers," September 25, 2007. www.marketwire.com.
Damian McNamara	"Momentum Builds for Addiction Medicine Specialty," *ACEP News*, August 2009. www.acep.org.
Kathy Walsh Nufer	"Getting Past Denial, Public Stigma First Battle in Alcohol Abuse Recovery," *Appleton (WI) Post-Crescent*, July 27, 2008.
Andrew Ryan	"In A&E's Gritty 'The Cleaner,' They're Not All Happy Endings," *Globe and Mail* (Toronto), July 15, 2008.
Linda Thomas	"College Students Report Benefits of Binge Drinking," MyNorthwest.com, July 6, 2011. www.mynorthwest.com.

OPPOSING
VIEWPOINTS®
SERIES

CHAPTER 4

Should Interventions Be Televised?

Chapter Preface

In recent years stories of individuals struggling in the throes of alcoholism and drug addiction have proven to be reliable television ratings magnets, guaranteed to attract large audiences. A&E's *Intervention*, for example, has been on the air since March of 2005 and is still going strong, due to its continuing ability to pull in viewers. Each episode of the show follows one or two individuals who have been nominated by their families or close friends as potential candidates for an intervention. (The form for nominating a friend or family member can be found on the A&E website: www.aetv.com/intervention/participate.) Believing their stories will become part of a documentary film and unaware of the fact that a televised intervention is being planned, selected subjects have allowed A&E cameras unlimited access to their lives. They have been filmed, often multiple times and in various situations, scoring drugs and shooting up, chugging down and vomiting, stealing a dying family member's painkillers, lying to their closest friends and their children in order to get a fix, and—on at least one occasion—operating a vehicle while under the influence.

Members of the intervention team are also filmed. Unlike the identified subjects of the episode, team members are fully aware of the nature of the project. Viewers of the show see them as they are educated about the nature of addiction as a disease process and encouraged to reflect on how it has insinuated itself into the life of someone they care about. They are also encouraged to examine how their own efforts to shield the subject from the consequences of his or her actions have, paradoxically, enabled a downward, self-destructive spiral.

Once the show's producers have fully explored, on camera, the extent of drug- or alcohol-induced pathology and the toll it has taken on the subject's life and relationships, the intervention begins. Often the results are good. At one point in 2011 producers of the show made the claim that of 194 interventions conducted on the series, 151 individuals were still successfully engaged in their recovery from addiction. The ratio has remained fairly constant, and it has been observed that the presence of cameras may actually contribute to the long-term success of the intervention process.

Still, the show has caused some to feel squeamish. "*Intervention* is . . . an exercise in fraud, as it fools its addicts into participating," according to Matthew Gilbert in the *Boston Globe* on March 5, 2005. "Unaware of the intervention theme, they've signed releases to be filmed for a show about addiction (an already questionable signature, since these shaky people aren't exactly of sound mind). Under false pretenses, they've been encouraged to expose their darkest behaviors to the cameras. Suddenly, in a bait-and-switch that seems like a media ambush, the addicts are confronted in an intervention, faced not only by friends and family but by the A&E cameras. In what could be the most decisive moment of their lives, they've been completely fooled. . . . Even if they later approve their participation in *Intervention*, the process of deception that preceded the final permission is repellent. No amount of inspirational reality TV can justify that kind of trick."

As Matthew Gilbert's comments demonstrate, shows that televise the intervention process raise a number of ethical questions: Is it morally acceptable to withhold information about the true purpose of the cameras when obtaining signed release forms? What is the responsibility of television producers and camera crews who become witnesses to behavior that has the potential to result in harm, either to the identified subject or to someone else? What ethical constraints, if any, should govern the decisions of producers about what is finally seen on TV? These are some of the questions that are debated in the following chapter.

"Intervention . . . is riveting . . . [and]
offers real drama—drama in the Greek
sense of the word: It's all fear and pity
and pathos."

Interventions Make
Good Television

Natasha Vargas-Cooper

*Natasha Vargas-Cooper is the Los Angeles correspondent for The
Awl, a website based in New York. In this viewpoint she argues that
A&E's* Intervention *makes for good television and provides help
for the addicts whose lives it features, many of whom have managed to stay sober since appearing on the show.*

As you read, consider the following questions:

1. How many addicts featured on *Intervention* have been
   able to avoid relapsing after completing rehab, according
   to the author?
2. What kind of training do Jeff VanVonderen and Candy
   Finnigan have that qualifies them to work as interventionists, as reported by Vargas-Cooper?
3. According to the author, what do the facilities featured on
   Intervention receive in return for complimentary treatment for the show's addicts?

Of the 161 addicts that have appeared on A&E's show *Intervention* in the past five years, 130 are sober today. There is no standard metric for recovery, but you take into account the high recidivism of drug offenders going back to jail, the chronic relapsing of people who have passed through state-based rehab programs, and anyone who has dealt with an addict in his or her personal life, the 71 percent recovery rate is, by any standard, astonishingly high. It is a number the producers of the show tout, not only because it's impressive, but because they believe it is accurate. After the participants go through the show and complete rehab, *Intervention* has a dedicated staff member to do check-ins with participants, put them in touch with other support groups, and send out sobriety birthday cards.

Intervention's alumni range from hardened alcoholics to young women with virulent eating disorders, with meth-heads, huffers, and full-blown opiate addicts in between. The show casts from a pool of the most dogged drug addicts, whose pathologies have wrought enough carnage in their lives that their families willingly collude with reality-TV show producers to lock their loved one in a room and demand they check into treatment under threat of banishment, homelessness, or jail while the cameras roll. So here is the obvious question: How has a 45-minute reality show that airs during summer on basic cable succeeded where so many other treatment regimes have failed? Why does a camera crew filming a determined drug addict hitting bottom convince someone to go into recovery? Does it merely take a united family leveling threats all at once to exorcise some of the demonic powers of addiction? In other words, what the hell is this show doing right?

Intervention Is Good Drama

Before we get into any discussion about the inner workings of the show, the quality of *Intervention* should be addressed. It is riveting. There is no need to qualify this assessment with a pejorative "for a reality-TV show." The only thing *Intervention* has in common with shows like *Real Housewives of New York City* or

Survivor is that it's unscripted. *Intervention* offers real drama—drama in the Greek sense of the word: It's all fear and pity and pathos. Instead of just documenting the annals of addiction and the humiliation people put themselves through in order to maintain it, the show instead focuses on the complicated ecosystems that sustain addiction: families. This focus is perhaps the key reason for the show's success as both documentary series and an outreach program.

"The truth is that most addicts, if it was up to them, do not have the resources to even be an addict," Jeff VanVonderen—one of the show's trained interventionists—tells me over the phone from his home in Orange County, California. "Somebody's gotta be paying something or putting up with something or ignoring something."

VanVonderen is a Level II (specialized in treating drugs, alcohol, gambling, and eating disorders) certified interventionist who also holds a degree from seminary school. VanVonderen is a Midwesterner, built like a linebacker, and a lapsed alcoholic himself. His counterpart on the show is Candy Finnigan, also a trained interventionist; Finnigan, a recovered addict, has big, soulful eyes and a social worker's disposition. VanVonderen, on the other hand, deals with addicts and their families as though he were coaching a football team getting whooped on its own turf.

When you are selected to be on *Intervention* you are tricked out of necessity. Participants are told they are subjects of a documentary series about addiction, which is essentially true, but what they are not told is that while they are holed up in their living rooms with a camera crew getting loaded, their family is preparing with producers for a filmed showdown. Once a subject is selected, *Intervention* researchers spend an average of two weeks compiling a psychological profile of the addict that's then reviewed by Finnigan and VanVonderen. The show also has a dedicated facility liaison, Jennifer Sneider, who chooses what kind of rehab the participant is sent to. She selects from a pool

True to Life

Television rarely gets any more real or dramatic than with A&E's #1 hit, *Intervention*, which delivers 2.0 million total viewers, 1.4 million Adults 18–49 and 1.3 million Adults 25–54 viewers each week. *Intervention* is a powerful and gripping series in which people confront their personal crises and seek a route to redemption. Its audience has grown considerably since its 2005 launch, rising 54% among total viewers and by even greater margins in the younger Adults 18–49 (+74%) and Adults 25–54 (+63%) demographics. In addition, the show has just received its second consecutive Emmy nomination as Outstanding Reality Series.

Nielsenwire, *September 7, 2009.*
http://blog.nielsen.com/nielsenwire.

of about a hundred facilities ranging in price from $50,000 to $120,000 for a 90-day stay, which is the minimum mandated by the show. The facilities give *Intervention* participants free stays in return for the free advertising. Sneider tries to line up the specialties of the treatment facilities to the patient profile.

Accurate Diagnosis Is Vital

This methodology seems to be one [of] the vital elements to the show's impressive sobriety rate: an accurate diagnosis. The 12-step method [a standard addiction recovery method], the thinking goes, wouldn't be very effective for a middle-aged mother with a busted back who subsists on a diet of prescription opiates to stave off crippling pain. Addiction, through her prism, is a small price to pay for relief from a twisted spinal column. The show would likely place her in a facility that specializes in chronic pain treatment and addiction, like Bay Recovery in San Diego. An adult male, on the other hand, who endured sexual molestation as child and now shoots heroin to ward off depression may be less likely to relapse if he were to be sent to a rehab facility that specializes in post-traumatic stress disorder. This latter case would be classified by *Intervention* and the treatment community as a "dual diagnosis."

A dual diagnosis is a person who is mentally ill and has a substance-abuse problem. "Those two things wrap around each other like a vine on a trellis," VanVonderen explains, "and if you tear one down and not the other, the other one comes back."

In the recovery community, controversy still swirls around treating addicts as though they have a disease. The disease model of addiction treatment advances the idea that, in an addict, there are genetic as well as environmental issues that create a chronic, sometimes life-long reliance on addictive substances if not addressed. But others have argued that addiction is just as simple as a faulty character or the power of the drug itself; meaning, if you could convince the person to just quit their preferred poison, many of their problems would solve themselves.

Dan Partland, *Intervention*'s executive producer, says that the show adopts the disease model philosophy of treatment. "I don't know if addiction is an actual disease or not, that's not my field," Partland says, "but treating addiction like it is a disease seems to work the best. So that's what we do."

Addicts' Families Receive Training

A key factor in the show's high recovery rate only gets about two minutes of air-time: the intervention training with the addict's loved ones. The trainings are six- to eight-hours long and are conducted by Finnigan or VanVonderen the day before the actual intervention. One part of the training is spent unearthing the various ways the family has been hurt by the addict's behavior, with the interventionist providing insight into the physiological science of addiction. But the majority of the time is spent dissembling the system that has enabled the addict to finance and feed their affliction. The family is forced to confront the great paradox of addiction: Enabling is the emotional infrastructure created to protect addicts from total self-destruction but ultimately empowers them to continue killing themselves. VanVonderen describes the training as an intervention on the family itself. The heart of the questions he often poses are: "Are you supporting something that you don't agree with? When you're paying the guy's rent, would you agree with them living with free rent so they can use their rent money for dope?"

According to VanVonderen, it's not hard to get an addict to agree to go to rehab during an intervention. When a family levels threats all at once, an addict will relent, but what they are actually trying to do is just get the threats to stop in the moment. Without some intensive pre-planning and commitment, the family has not changed the way it operates and, VanVonderen says, "That's a formula for relapse."

After the intervention is filmed and the participant goes directly to rehab, their treatment will last a minimum of 90 days. That is a relatively new precedent in the treatment industry, where the standard has generally been 28 days. When people qualify for state-funded recovery programs or are ordered to go to rehab by the courts, the state will only pay for 28 days. However, now more rehab programs are instituting 90-day treatment regimes because they are thought to yield better results. The idea is that 'drying out,' or not using, for 28 days could get you clean, but it won't keep you sober; simply weaning the body off substances is not enough. Treatment under the 90-day model is considered to be cumulative; the eighth week has a bigger impact than the fourth week. The production team, including the interventionists, say that it's the show that has influenced the wide adoption of the 90-day program. (Lindsay Lohan will be the most recent and high-profile beneficiary of this evolving philosophy in treatment.)

Interventions Lead to Recovery

So what role do the cameras play in this road to recovery? Is that another element in the show's successful treatment rate? According to VanVonderen, no. "It's not because of the show that people have broken through their addiction—I think it's because of the intervention. People are more likely to go to treatment if there's an intervention, they're more likely to stay in treatment, they're more likely to do better afterward, because everything's changed. Not just, they went to treatment. The family's gonna get well without you, and that comes through in the intervention."

In other words, VanVonderen says the real power of the intervention comes through when addicts learn, "Now the jig is up, it's not gonna work like it did before. That strikes fear into their hearts."

> "Public drama—though great for TV—is
> not the place for the private trauma
> most families experience when a loved
> one has a serious addiction or mental
> health disorder."

Interventions Do Not Belong on Television

Louise Stanger

In this viewpoint Louise Stanger, a licensed clinical social worker who specializes in substance abuse and mental health issues, describes the intervention process. She contends that televising such events is wrong because it is unethical to expose addicts and their families to public scrutiny while they are involved in an intervention.

As you read, consider the following questions:

1. What is the overall purpose of an intervention, according to Stanger?
2. What is the secondary benefit of an intervention, in the author's opinion?
3. Why is Stanger critical of the TV show *Intervention?*

An intervention in all of its many forms and iterations is an invitation for clients and their families to seek health care treatment so that their lives may be enriched. While much has been written and talked about on TV, licensed mental health and health providers do interventions every day in residential settings, crisis clinics, government offices, private practices and hospital settings. We as licensed professionals (MDs, general and Psychiatrists, Certified Alcohol Counselors, Certified Rehabilitation Counselors, Psychologists, Nurses, Licensed Clinical Social Workers, Licensed Marriage and Family Counselors) are always inviting our clients to explore ways to improve their lives. We try to empower them to be the captains of their well-being. An intervention is merely an invitation to seek additional care. Viewed in this way, it does not become a drama, but rather a reality of everyday practice.

An intervention is a highly stylized process that helps everyone involved accept that the person they value, care about and love has a serious problem. It may be diagnosed as a substance abuse disorder (alcohol, legal drugs, illegal drugs), or a process addiction disorder (food, sex, gambling, debt) and/or a mental health disorder (depression, bi-polar, mania, borderline). In acknowledging this fact, participants learn about the nature of the disorder—its etiology, history, and progression—and learn to understand that it's a disease similar to medical conditions like diabetes and heart disease.

The overall purpose of an intervention is to create an opening in the denial system of the Identified Patient (IP) and to facilitate getting help for this person. The secondary benefit is family and friends learning new ways of relating to one another and taking care of themselves. This is accomplished by helping the IP and everyone involved accept the difficult reality of the current situation. Treatment options are then explored and arrangements are made for the IP to accept the treatment being offered. Family interventions are difficult and delicate matters. Anger and profound sorrow often result when someone is forced

Professionals Worry About Exploitation

Some professionals in the rehab field worry that programs about addiction—a genre that includes HBO's documentary series *Addiction* and A&E's popular *Intervention*, now in its 10th season—are exploiting patients in their most vulnerable moments. Sure, participants are getting free treatment, but there's also a concern that cameras interfere with the process.

Amy Kaufman, Los Angeles Times, January 2, 2011.

to look at his or her own behavior. Family members often experience mournful rage, deep sadness and guilt over failed efforts. It is imperative for a professional to be present to help coach you along the way. As a professional interventionist, I've learned that a safe, comfortable, and respectful atmosphere is essential for success.

While all persons in a family share traits and mannerisms, each person is different; each is unique. And each requires different tools and strategies to help the patient and themselves heal. I carefully assess each person's needs, being mindful of trauma and other mental health issues. Then provide skills that facilitate growth.

After careful coaching, planning, and wise deliberation, the intervention is conducted in a loving, caring manner in which all participants come together for a common cause—helping their loved one get treatment. In doing so, they strengthen their respect for each other and the patient.

Lastly is the follow-up process. While the IP is in treatment, I provide case management services with the treatment center.

I continue to work with the family providing Solution-Focused Coaching and help them discover a plan for their own healing. I can also provide support and guidance during the transition from treatment to home or new living situation.

What an Intervention Is Not

Interventions are not like the scenarios played out on television screens. As a licensed professional, I believe the TV show *Intervention* turns the despair and pain of families faced with addiction, and turns it all into a soap opera. I assure you that doing a confidential intervention is very different than what you see on TV. There are no cameras lurking in the background trying to catch your loved one shooting up or engaging in harmful activities and other indiscretions. Based on my professional training, I believe that's unethical. Confidentiality and discretion is paramount. Finding the best treatment centers available is my task. Your task is choosing the one that fits best and is most likely to create positive change.

Lastly, public drama—though great for TV—is not the place for the private trauma most families experience when a loved one has a serious addiction or mental health disorder. Interventions are not group or individual counseling. Loved ones come together for a singular, specific purpose—to help the identified patient. When other semi-related but not central issues come up, I refer participants to therapists, doctors and self-help groups for more intensive counseling.

Interventions are not everyone talking at once. An intervention is not a free-for-all. You are taught a highly stylized way of communicating. Any individual sessions for participants are part of the assessment process, not the actual intervention.

Interventions are not conducted when a person is intoxicated, under the influence, suicidal, known to be violent, extremely depressed, in mania, or suffering from another serious mental health disorder. Cases are carefully assessed to confirm that this method is the right approach. For example, extra precautions must be taken when doing an intervention on a male patient with a history of violent acting out. Or when a patient is addicted to cocaine and is also in a manic stage. Or when a young girl is suffering from both anorexia and depression.

> "Legally, producers are treated like
> witnesses: they bear no responsibility to
> intervene."

The Producer of *Intervention* Was Not Legally Obligated to Prevent an Impaired Person from Driving

Jeremy W. Peters

In this viewpoint Jeremy W. Peters, a media reporter for the New York Times, *examines the legal responsibilities connected with the production of reality TV shows and contends that the producer of* Intervention *was not legally bound to prevent a cast member from driving after drinking.*

As you read, consider the following questions:

1. Why, according to the author, is it usually difficult to make a case for negligence against producers of a reality TV show?
2. What does an accusing party have to show in order to prove that producers of a reality TV show are guilty of negligence, according to Peters?

3. What two examples of lawsuits in which networks settled cases privately does the author mention?

O n a recent episode of *Intervention*, A&E's documentary series about addiction, no one was stopping Pam, an alcoholic, from driving.

As she made her way to the front door—stopping first at the refrigerator to take a swig of vodka for the road—viewers could hear a producer for the show speak up.

"You have had a lot to drink," the voice from off camera said. "Do you want one of us to drive?"

Pam was indignant. "No, I can drive. I can drive," she mumbled. She then got into her car, managed a three-point turn out of the parking lot and drove off. The camera crew followed, filming her as she tried to keep her turquoise Pontiac Sunfire between the lines.

Perhaps more than any other program on television now, *Intervention* highlights the sticky situations that reality-show producers can find themselves in as they document unpredictable and unstable subjects or situations. In recent years, producers and networks have increasingly pushed the boundaries of television voyeurism in search of another ratings hit.

Lawsuits Have Occurred

At times, this has proved problematic for television networks. There have been several lawsuits related to shows like *Big Brother* and more recently, CBS found itself facing accusations that it had created dangerous working conditions for children in its reality program *Kid Nation*, in which children aged 8 to 15 toiled in the New Mexico desert to build a working society on their own.

In the case of reality-TV documentary shows like *Intervention* and the various incarnations of *The Real World* and *Road Rules* on MTV, producers can be witnesses to crimes, raising the question of when they are obligated to step out from behind the camera and intervene.

Sometimes the crimes they film are relatively minor, like underage drinking or fisticuffs. But in other cases, like on *Intervention* and VH1's *Breaking Bonaduce,* in which the star, the former child actor Danny Bonaduce, got behind the wheel after he had been drinking and bragged how a car crash would make great television, the program's subjects can put themselves and innocent bystanders at great risk.

And legally, producers are treated like witnesses: they bear no responsibility to intervene.

"The law in the United States doesn't require you to step in and save people," said David Sternbach, counsel for litigation and intellectual property matters for A&E Television Networks. "And it doesn't require you to stop a crime that's in the works."

Often, of course, they have good business reasons not to: people on the edge make for good television. *Intervention* is one of A&E's top shows. This year [2007] it has drawn up to two million viewers on its best nights. The premiere of *Kid Nation* attracted 9.1 million viewers but slipped the next week to 7.6 million.

The first season of *Breaking Bonaduce* helped VH1 increase its prime-time ratings in 2005, though they faded in the second season. And a wide following for *Cops,* Fox's police ride-along reality show, has kept it on the air since 1989.

Making a Case Would Be Difficult

A&E said *Intervention* has never been sued. And legal experts said that making a case against it or other documentary programs like it would be difficult because the subjects were being filmed in their own homes, engaging in activities that they would be pursuing regardless of whether a camera crew was there.

"This is their life with me or without me," said Sam Mettler, *Intervention's* creator and executive producer. The program takes other steps, like requiring potential subjects to undergo psychological evaluations and keeping a family member of the addict on call 24 hours a day during filming, to avoid being negligent.

To make a case for negligence, legal experts said, the accusing party would need to prove that the reality program created a situation that put its subjects in jeopardy. A *Big Brother* cast member sued CBS, for example, in 2002 after another cast member with a criminal record held a knife to her throat. CBS settled the case for an undisclosed amount.

When the sister of a woman who appeared on ABC's *Extreme Makeover* committed suicide in 2004, the contestant sued the network for wrongful death and other charges. The contestant, who was competing to win free plastic surgery but lost, claimed that her sister had felt so guilty about mocking her appearance on the program that she killed herself. ABC settled the case for an undisclosed amount last year [2006].

Producers Are Not Policemen

But if a subject on a show like *Intervention* or Fox's *Cops* series were to injure someone while engaging in illegal activity, a case for negligence would be more difficult to make because producers are merely observing.

"Television producers are not policemen," said Michael J. O'Connor, whose firm White O'Connor Curry in Los Angeles, Calif., has represented reality shows like *Survivor* and *America's Next Top Model.* He added: "On a moral level, you get to the point where stepping in seems like it would be something you'd want to do. But from a legal standpoint, third parties causing injuries to other third parties is not something a television program is really responsible for."

Being absolved of legal responsibility for his documentary subjects, however, does not make shooting the program any easier.

"I've had children of alcoholic parents there watching their mother in a drunken stupor, watching their mother pass out, watching their mother throw up," Mr. Mettler said. "Those innocent children as casualties of their mother's addiction was just emotionally heart-wrenching. The trauma of that is horrible, just horrible."

Producers Must Provide a Safe Work Environment

Reality show contestants participating in reality shows which contain challenges, situations, or events that pose a peculiar risk of physical harm have a good chance of trumping any assumption of the risk defense. Producers must provide an environment free from the peculiar risk of harm associated with the challenges. This is a non-delegable duty. Producers cannot ignore their duty to provide a safe working environment simply by having their participants/independent contractors agree to their waiver of this responsibility.

Kelley Tiffany, Employee Relations Law Journal, *Summer 2006.*

Real People in Their Real Lives

Intervention, which ends each episode with an actual intervention, has arrangements with substance-abuse rehabilitation centers across the country that provide free in-patient treatment for addicts on the program.

"Morally and ethically, none of us can feel good watching someone hurt themselves or hurt someone else. And I'm not going to stand by and have someone who is drunk get behind the wheel of a car and kill someone," Mr. Mettler said.

Mr. Mettler himself has had to step out from behind the camera on a number of episodes to prevent someone from driving drunk. In one case, he followed a crack addict named Tim through a swamp. Tim had crawled into a drainage pipe and threatened suicide, so Mr. Mettler had to talk him out.

And in another episode, Mr. Mettler's field producers called paramedics after an alcoholic they were filming overdosed on the sedative trazodone. Laney, a wealthy divorced woman who drank half a gallon of rum a day and traveled long distances in limousines because she did not like putting her cat on commercial jets, swallowed the pills while the cameras were off. She told producers what she had done after they saw her chugging a bottle of juice to wash the pills down.

"Our first position is that this is a documentary series, we are there capturing real people in their real lives," said Robert Sharenow, A&E's senior vice president for nonfiction and alternative programming. "If there was an immediate danger, that was sort of our line. If the person was putting themselves or anyone else in immediate danger, then we'd cross the line."

He added: "It's a very, very delicate balance."

> "When you encounter an inebriated person who is about to go for a drive, you may not legally be required to get involved, but ethically you are, even if you are a producer of reality TV shows."

The Producer of *Intervention* Was Ethically Obligated to Prevent an Impaired Person from Driving

Bruce Weinstein

Bruce Weinstein is a corporate consultant and public speaker known as The Ethics Guy. In this viewpoint he argues that although reality show producers are not legally required to prevent their shows' subjects from harming themselves or others, they are ethically required to do so.

As you read, consider the following questions:

1. According to the author, what three meaningful questions should be asked not only about reality show scenarios but also in real-life situations?

2. What are some of the distinctions Weinstein makes between legal penalties and ethical penalties?
3. Why does the author believe that ethical standards are more important than legal ones?

Imagine that you are producing a reality TV series about alcoholism. You like the cinéma vérité approach (otherwise known as the "fly on the wall" school of filmmaking), so you have your crew follow the routine of a woman, Pam, who is struggling with this disease. At one point, Pam decides to go for a drive. Before leaving the house, Pam takes a swig of vodka. She is in no position to get behind the wheel, so you ask her if she would like for someone in the crew to assist her.

She mumbles, "No, I can drive," and heads out to her Pontiac Sunbird. Fearing that the woman could be a danger to herself and others, you prevent her from getting into her car and turning it into a killing machine, right? Wrong. You let her drive off.

WHAT?

Well, according to an article in the Oct. 8 issue of the *New York Times* (NYT), this is actually how a member of the team responsible for the A&E program, *Intervention*, responded to the situation. As disturbing as the choice to do nothing is, the *Times* notes that "legally, producers are treated like witnesses: They bear no responsibility to intervene." Consider the following statement from Michael J. O'Connor, an attorney who has represented reality shows such as *Survivor* and *America's Next Top Model*, as quoted in the *Times*:

"Television producers are not policemen. On a moral level, you get to the point where stepping in seems like it would be something you'd want to do. But from a legal standpoint, third parties causing injuries to other third parties is not something a television program is really responsible for."

O'Connor's statement raises three meaningful questions that apply not just to the world of TV but to the world at large:

- Are our responsibilities limited to what the law requires of us?
- If we are legally allowed to do something, does that mean we ought to?
- If there is no relevant law to speak of with respect to a "What should I do?" problem we're facing, does that mean that anything goes?

The answers to these questions are: No. No. No.

Ethics vs. the Law

Imagine that you are at the end of your life and you are looking back on all you did and didn't do over the years. Imagine also that your life was dedicated primarily to satisfying your own needs and desires. When faced with the question, "What should I do?," you inevitably chose the solution that benefited you in some way, no matter how this choice affected others. How would you evaluate a life lived in this fashion?

Even if it was the case that you never broke any laws, you cannot say that you lived your best life, because life should not be solely about "me, myself, and I." To be fully human and be a part of civilized society means to go beyond what the law demands of us. It means to live according to ethical rules and principles, many of which ask more of us than the law does. The answer to "What should I do?" should therefore not be, "What can I get away with legally?" but "What does ethics ask or even require of me?"

There are other differences between ethics and the law. Laws change over time. Laws vary from state to state. Most significantly, political and economic interests, and not the interests of the people, often determine which laws get passed and what is in those laws. Ethical standards, however, transcend time, place, and the whims of politics.

Forms of Punishment

For example, when you encounter an inebriated person who is about to go for a drive, you may not legally be required to get involved, but ethically you are, even if you are a producer of reality TV shows. It is no defense to say, as *Intervention* Executive Producer Sam Mettler does in the *Times* article, that "this is their life with me or without me." As soon as you show up with a camera, you are ethically implicated in the choices your subject makes.

In fact, simply by being an observer, you are ethically accountable for what happens on your watch. To be a member of the human race is to care for what transpires in the world around us. It is hard to imagine how any law could demand that we care for strangers or require punishment if we don't. This is the proper role, however, of ethics. The penalty for violating an ethical requirement may not involve a prison term, but it can involve scorn or ridicule from others, or feelings of guilt or shame for having let ourselves down or disappointed our family and friends. All of these are forms of punishment just the same.

In 1965, Hebrew National playfully seized upon the split between our legal and ethical responsibilities when it coined the slogan, "We answer to a higher authority." They were on to something. Whether it's cold cuts for lunch, a reliable computer for work, or a safe toy for your child, don't you want the companies with which you do business to go beyond merely what the law requires of them and be the very best they can be?

From the Pages of History

Let's delve more deeply into the schism between ethics and the law. Consider the following facts from U.S. history:

- Slavery was perfectly legal until the 13th Amendment to the Constitution abolished it in 1865.
- Children were allowed to work in mines, glass factories, and textile and other industries instead of going to school until the Fair Labor Standards Act was passed in 1938.
- Women didn't have the right to vote until 1920.

• On Dec. 1, 1955, in Montgomery, Ala., Rosa Parks broke the law when she refused to give up her bus seat to a white passenger.

How is it possible that a practice that was legal in the past is now against the law? Is it the case that slavery, for example, used to be ethical, but now it isn't? Of course not. Ethics hasn't changed. The law just took awhile to become aligned with what is right.

Although business as an institution has been getting a bad rap in the mainstream media for the wrongful conduct committed at Enron, Adelphia, WorldCom, Tyco (TYC), and other companies, let's not forget those organizations that took the high road, went beyond what the law required of them, and ultimately reaped many rewards. For example, in 1982, seven people in the Chicago area died of cyanide poisoning after unwittingly consuming tainted Tylenol capsules. Within a matter of days, Johnson & Johnson (JNJ) responded aggressively by withdrawing all 31 million bottles of the drug (with a retail value of over $100 million), creating a new, triple-sealed package, and offering consumers deep discounts.

Effectively and Ethically Managing a Crisis

The law did not require Johnson & Johnson to take such measures, but by doing so, the company earned the respect of consumers and the media alike, and this case is now widely taught in business schools as an example of how to manage a crisis effectively—and continue to prosper. Those seven who died can never be brought back, but J&J took extraordinary steps to ensure that no one else would be in jeopardy. Here we are, 25 years after the fact, still talking about how the company conducted itself admirably. (Disclosure: Several years ago, I gave a few speeches that were sponsored by Vistakon, a subsidiary of Johnson & Johnson.)

For any law, we can and should ask: Is it right? Is it fair? Is it just?

The ultimate standards for deciding what we ought to do are ethical, not legal, ones. As the *Intervention* example shows, sometimes we are not legally obligated to do what we ought to do. Our history of failing to recognize the inherent dignity of women, children, and African-Americans shows that the law sometimes gets it all wrong. And the Tylenol case suggests that companies that value doing the right thing rather than what is merely legally required of them may not only endure, but prevail. As this column has endeavored to show over and over, the reason to do the right thing is simply because it is the right thing to do. Businesses that take ethics seriously, however, often find themselves winning over consumers and a skeptical media alike.

We are a nation of laws, and our society would quickly devolve into anarchy without the rule of law as a binding, motivating force for all of us. Nevertheless, the ethical principles of "Do No Harm" (*BusinessWeek*, 1/10/07), "Make Things Better" (*BusinessWeek*, 1/18/07); "Respect Others" (*BusinessWeek*, 1/25/07), "Be Fair" (*BusinessWeek*, 2/8/07), and "Be Loving" (*BusinessWeek*, 2/22/07) are the true basis of our society, and it is to those principles we ought to return every day when we ask ourselves: "What should I do? What kind of person should I be? How can I bring out the best in myself and others?"

Yes, laws are important. But all of us, and not just the employees of a certain manufacturer of hot dogs and salami, should answer to a higher authority.

Periodical and Internet Sources Bibliography

The following articles have been selected to supplement the diverse views presented in this chapter.

Ginia Bellafante	"They Drink, They Drug, and You Are There," *New York Times*, August 17, 2008.
Mike Gellman	"I Saw You on *Intervention*," *Huffington Post*, October 7, 2010.
Jim Halterman	"Interview: 'Intervention's' Candy Finnigan & Jeff VanVonderen," *Futon Critic* (blog), December 13, 2010. http://twitter.com/#!/thefutoncritic.
John Hines	"Reality Shows Need an Intervention," *Volante Online* (University of South Dakota), November 10, 2010.
Rick Ingebritson	"'Rescue Me' Shows How Not to Stage an Intervention," *Palm Beach (FL) Post*, July 22, 2009.
Jason R. Kosovski and Douglas C. Smith	"Everybody Hurts: Addiction, Drama and the Family in the Reality Television Show *Intervention*," *Substance Use and Misuse*, May 2011.
Michel Martin	"Former Addict Helps Families of the Afflicted," National Public Radio, March 17, 2010. www.npr.org.
Mary-Ann McBride	"What's On Tonight," *Albuquerque (NM) Tribune*, March 16, 2011.
Evelyn Theiss	"This Ain't No Reality Show: PDQ's 10 Minutes with Interventionist Jane Eigner Mintz," *Cleveland Plain Dealer*, November 5, 2008.
G. Wright	"'Intervention' Creator Sam Mettler Talks to Social Workers," Social Workers Speak, February 16, 2010. www.socialworkersspeak.org.

For Further Discussion

Chapter 1

1. The author of the first viewpoint in this chapter, Elaine Appleton Grant, believes baby boomers are less susceptible to feelings of shame about addiction than earlier generations were, and are thus more likely to be open about their substance abuse problems and to seek treatment. How is this similar to or different from attitudes toward drug and alcohol abuse on college campuses that are described in the second viewpoint by UniversityChic.com?

2. Do you view feelings of shame as having a positive or a negative effect on a person's ability to confront a personal substance abuse problem? Explain your answer citing from the viewpoints.

3. Why, according to James Schuster, is the workplace a good place to confront an individual about his or her abuse of drugs or alcohol? Do you agree or disagree? Why?

Chapter 2

1. What is it about "the Johnson method," as described by Sarah Kershaw, that lends itself to the television reality show format?

2. What is harm reduction? Do you think harm reduction is an acceptable therapeutic goal and a realistic alternative to intervention and recovery? Explain, citing from the viewpoints.

Chapter 3

1. According to Vernon Johnson, as cited in the viewpoint by Nancy Doyle Palmer, the individuals who are closest to the person who has a substance abuse problem are the best ones to have on an intervention team. Why is this?

2. Who do you think could most effectively address a person's denial about a drinking problem: his or her spouse or employer? Why?

3. Do you think a family member's anger could interfere with his or her ability to participate in an intervention? Explain your answer.

Chapter 4

1. On the show *Intervention*, the standard amount of time spent in rehabilitation is ninety days. Most people cannot realistically expect to stay in rehab for that length of time. The typical amount of time is twenty-eight days. Which do you think has the better chance of success? Explain, citing from the viewpoints.

2. Do you think the show *Intervention* creates false expectations, since the treatment it offers is not available to most people? Why or why not?

3. What positive values, if any, do you see in the kind of personal sharing that takes place when interventions are televised? Explain.

Organizations to Contact

The editors have compiled the following list of organizations concerned with the issues debated in this book. The descriptions are derived from materials provided by the organizations. All have publications or information available for interested readers. The list was compiled on the date of publication of the present volume; the information provided here may change. Be aware that many organizations take several weeks or longer to respond to inquiries, so allow as much time as possible.

The Abbey Foundation
1401 Central Ave.
Bettendorf, IA 52722
(563) 355-4707 • fax: (563) 355-7647
e-mail: info@theabbeyfoundation.org
website: www.theabbeyfoundation.org

The Abbey Foundation is a nonprofit organization dedicated to battling addiction through research, prevention, and financial aid for those in need of treatment. Its members produce articles related to addiction that are available on the website, such as "Substance Abuse Treatment and the Baby Boomer Population."

Al-Anon Family Group/Alateen
1600 Corporate Landing Pkwy.
Virginia Beach, VA 23454
(757) 563-1600; toll-free: (888) 4AL-ANON
fax: (757) 563-1655
e-mail: wso@al-anon.org
website: www.al-anon.alateen.org

Al-Anon provides support and encouragement to relatives and friends of individuals with an alcohol problem. Its program is adapted from the 12 Steps of Alcoholics Anonymous. Alateen is a program geared for teenagers and sometimes for younger children. Al-Anon has published more than a hundred books and pamphlets and produces a monthly magazine, the *Forum*.

Alcoholics Anonymous (AA)
PO Box 459, Grand Central Station
New York, NY 10163
(212) 870-3400
website: www.aa.org

AA is an independent worldwide fellowship for support and encouragement for anyone who wants to stop drinking and maintain sobriety. The website contains extensive information for the public, including information about alcoholism, how to find nearby AA meetings, and how to find a treatment facility. Publications are available online, including the *Alcoholics Anonymous Big Book*, the basic text of AA; *Twelve Steps and Twelve Traditions*; and *AA Grapevine*, the online multimedia journal of AA.

The Association for Addiction Professionals (NAADAC)
1001 N. Fairfax Street, Suite 201
Alexandria, VA 22314
(800) 548-0497 • fax: (800) 377-1136
website: www.naadac.org

NAADAC is a membership organization serving addiction counselors, educators, and other addiction-focused health care professionals who specialize in addiction prevention, treatment, recovery support, and education. Its website includes information about addiction science, resources for individuals, and certification programs for substance abuse professionals. The organization publishes the magazine *Addiction Professional* and *NAADAC Newsletter*.

Association of Intervention Specialists (AIS)
313 W. Liberty Street, Suite 129
Lancaster, PA 17603
(717) 392-8488
website: http://associationofinterventionspecialists.org

The Association of Intervention Specialists is a network of interventionists located throughout the country and abroad. Members are board-certified interventionists who meet or exceed educational and performance standards. The AIS website includes a code of ethics and sections titled *What Is an Intervention?* and *What Is an Interventionist?* that contain information on training and other requirements for earning board certification.

Intervention Resource Center, Inc.
1028 Barret Ave.
Louisville, KY 40204
(502) 451-4772; toll-free: (888) 421-4321
fax: (502) 451-1334
e-mail: help@interventioninfo.org
website: www.interventioninfo.org

The Intervention Resource Center, Inc. is a not-for-profit organization focused on helping alcoholics and other drug-addicted persons and their families and employers overcome the pain and economic costs associated with addiction. The center provides referral to intervention and treatment programs, and its website includes an extensive list of references aimed at increasing understanding of addiction, as well as various treatment options.

Narcotics Anonymous (NA)
PO Box 9999
Van Nuys, CA 91409
(818) 773-9999 • fax: (818) 700-0700
website: www.na.org

Narcotics Anonymous is a twelve-step recovery program for drug addicts. While modeled on other twelve-step programs, it is independent. Members support one another in learning how to live without drugs. NA publishes the *NA Way Magazine,* a recovery and service magazine for members, as well as other periodicals and reports such as *NA World Service News Reaching Out,* and NAWS annual reports.

The National Center on Addiction and Substance Abuse (CASA) at Columbia University

633 Third Ave., 19th Floor
New York, NY 10017-6706
(212) 841-5200
website: www.casacolumbia.org

The National Center on Addiction and Substance Abuse at Columbia University is a science-based, multidisciplinary organization focused on improving society's understanding of and responses to substance use and the disease of addiction. Its website includes educational resources, a newsroom, and information about organizations involved in substance abuse treatment and recovery. CASA produces books, reports, papers, and newsletters, such as *Women Under the Influence* and *Adolescent Substance Use: America's #1 Public Health Problem.*

National Institute on Alcohol Abuse and Alcoholism (NIAAA)

5635 Fishers Lane, MSC 9304
Bethesda, MD 20892-9304
(301) 443-3860
website: www.niaaa.nih.gov

The National Institute on Alcohol Abuse and Alcoholism, part of the National Institutes of Health, is an agency of the US government. NIAAA's mission is to support and promote the best science on alcohol and health by increasing the understanding of normal and abnormal biological functions and behavior relating to alcohol use and to improving the diagnosis, prevention, and treatment of alcohol use disorders. The NIAAA website includes information on current research, as well as recent press releases and educational materials. It publishes a quarterly bulletin, *Alcohol Alert,* and a quarterly, peer-reviewed scientific journal, *Alcohol Research & Health.*

National Institute on Drug Abuse (NIDA)
6001 Executive Blvd., Room 5213
Bethesda, MD 20892-9561
(301) 443-1124
e-mail: info@nida.nih.gov
website: www.nida.nih.gov

NIDA, part of the National Institutes of Health, is a US government agency that provides strategic support for scientific research on addiction and treatment and organizes and communicates the results of that research to improve prevention and treatment and to inform policy as it relates to drug abuse and addiction. The NIDA website includes a section for students and young adults. NIDA disseminates its research through such publications as the bimonthly *NIDA Notes* and *NIDA NewsScan*.

The Partnership at Drugfree.org
352 Park Ave. South, 9th Floor
New York, NY 10010
(212) 922-1560 • fax: (212) 922-1570
website: www.drugfree.org

The Partnership at Drugfree.org, formerly Partnership for a Drug-Free America, is a nonprofit educational organization that helps parents prevent, intervene in, and find treatment for drug and alcohol use by their children. The website includes information about specific drugs, including cocaine/crack, heroin, meth, ecstasy, marijuana. and prescription drugs. Among other reports, the organization publishes the annual Partnership Attitude Tracking Study (PATS), the longest-running national research study of parent and teen behaviors and attitudes about drug and alcohol use in the United States.

Substance Abuse and Mental Health Services Administration (SAMHSA)
1 Choke Cherry Road
Rockville, MD 20857

(877) 726-4727 • fax: (240) 221-4292
e-mail: samhsainfo@samhsa.hhs.gov
website: www.samhsa.gov

The Substance Abuse and Mental Health Services Administration's mission is to reduce the impact of substance abuse and mental illness in the United States. The SAMHSA website includes extensive resources on substance abuse treatment, prevention and recovery, for both laypersons and professionals. The SAMHSA website also includes a Substance Abuse Treatment Facility Locator at http://dasis3.samhsa.gov. *SAMHSA News* is its national bimonthly newsletter.

Secular Organizations for Sobriety (SOS)
The Center for Inquiry–Los Angeles
4773 Hollywood Blvd.
Los Angeles, CA 90027
(323) 666-4295
e-mail: sos@cfiwest.org
website: www.cfiwest.org/sos

Secular Organizations for Sobriety (SOS) is a recovery program for those alcoholics or drug addicts who are uncomfortable with the spiritual content of traditional twelve-step programs. SOS credits the individual for achieving and maintaining his or her own sobriety. The organization also supports scientific skepticism and encourages the use of the scientific method to understand alcoholism. The SOS National Clearinghouse publishes a quarterly newsletter.

Women for Sobriety (WFS)
PO Box 618
Quakertown, PA 18951-0618
(215) 536-8026; toll-free: (800) 333-1606
fax: (215) 538-9026
website: www.womenforsobriety.org

Women for Sobriety is an abstinence-based self-help program for women facing issues of alcohol or drug addiction. Its purpose is to help women find their individual paths to recovery through discovery of self, in conversation with other women in similar circumstances. Literature and an e-newsletter are available at its website.

Bibliography of Books

Linda Bickerstaff   *Cocaine: Coke and the War on Drugs.* New York: Rosen, 2009.

Stephanie L. Brooke   *The Use of the Creative Therapies with Chemical Dependency Issues.* Springfield, IL: Thomas, 2009.

Nancy D. Campbell, J.P. Olsen, and Luke Corydon Walden   *The Narcotic Farm.* New York: Abrams, 2008.

Tom Farley and Tanner Colby   *The Chris Farley Show: A Biography in Three Acts.* New York: Viking, 2008.

Jack E. Henningfield, Patricia B. Santora, and Warren K. Bickel   *Addiction Treatment: Science and Policy for the Twenty-First Century.* Baltimore: Johns Hopkins University Press, 2007.

John Hoffman and Susan Froemke, eds.   *Addiction: Why Can't They Just Stop? New Knowledge, New Treatments, New Hope.* Emmaus, PA: Rodale, 2007.

Debra Jay   *No More Letting Go: The Spirituality of Taking Action Against Alcoholism and Drug Addiction.* New York: Bantam Books, 2006.

Jeff Jay and Debra Jay   *Love First: A Family's Guide to Intervention.* Center City, MN: Hazelden, 2008.

Vernon E. Johnson	*Everything You Need to Know About Chemical Dependence: Vernon Johnson's Complete Guide for Families.* Center City, MN: Hazelden, 1990.
Vernon E. Johnson	*I'll Quit Tomorrow.* San Francisco: Harper & Row, 1980.
Vernon E. Johnson	*Intervention: How to Help Someone Who Doesn't Want Help.* Minneapolis: Johnson Institute Books, 1986.
Steven B. Karch	*Addiction and the Medical Complications of Drug Abuse.* Boca Raton, FL: CRC Press, 2008.
Kyle Keegan and Howard Moss	*Chasing the High: A Firsthand Account of One Young Person's Experience with Substance Abuse.* New York: Oxford University Press, 2008.
Peter M. Miller	*Evidence-Based Addiction Treatment.* Amsterdam: Elsevier/ Academic Press, 2009.
Alex Mold	*Heroin: The Treatment of Addiction in Twentieth-Century Britain.* Dekalb: Northern Illinois University Press, 2008.
William Cope Moyers and Katherine Ketcham	*Broken: My Story of Addiction and Redemption.* New York: Viking, 2006.
National Center on Addiction and Substance Abuse at Columbia University	*Women Under the Influence.* Baltimore: Johns Hopkins University Press, 2006.

Frank Owen

No Speed Limit: The Highs and Lows of Meth. New York: St. Martin's, 2007.

David Sheff

Beautiful Boy: A Father's Journey Through His Son's Addiction. Thorndike, ME: Center Point, 2008.

Joanne S. Stevenson and Marilyn Sawyer Sommers

Alcohol Use, Misuse, Abuse and Dependence. New York: Springer, 2006.

Harold Urschel

Curing the Addicted Brain: The Revolutionary, Science-Based Alcoholism and Addiction Recovery Program. Naperville, IL: Sourcebooks, 2009.

Bill W.

Alcoholics Anonymous: The Story of How Many Thousands of Men and Women Have Recovered from Alcoholism. New York: Alcoholics Anonymous World Services, 1976.

Andrew T. Wainwright and Robert Poznanovich

It's Not Okay to Be a Cannibal: How to Keep Addiction from Eating Your Family Alive. Center City, MN: Hazelden, 2007.

Laurence Michael Westreich

Helping the Addict You Love: The New Effective Program for Getting the Addict into Treatment. New York: Fireside, 2007.

Index

Pam (alcoholic), 147, 153
Parents, 21, 49
Parks, Rosa, 156
Partland, Dan, 138
Partnership for a Drug-Free
America, 110
Partying, 33
Personal choices, 57, 59–61
Peters, Jeremy W., 146–151
Phillips, Melanie, 81
Podcasts, 72
Police, 75
Polydrug users, 89
Poznanovich, Bob, 96–102, 105,
106
Prescription Drug Take-Back, 20
Prescription drugs, 20, 21, 67, 69
Prevention, 59, 87, 88
Principles, 157
Prism Award, 15
Problem solving skills, 118, 119
Process addiction disorders, 142
Producers, reality TV programs,
150, 153
Productivity, 38, 39
Propofol, 68
Punishment, 155

Q
Quest Diagnostics, 43–45
Quest Diagnostics Drug Testing
Index (DTI), 43–45
Quitting, 52, 53, 60

R
Random drug testing, 44, 45
Real Housewives of New York City
(TV program), 135
Reality television, 16, 135, 150
See also individual TV
programs
The Real World (TV program), 147
Recovery

for family members, 116–18
family support in, 118–20
of *Intervention* TV program
participants, 135
loss of, 115
Red Chair (company), 75–76
Referral fees, 76
Regulatory authority, 126
Rehab programs, 25, 26, 29, 30,
136–39
Relapse
family hope and, 115
family support and, 139
management, 53, 89–90
prevention therapy, 59, 87, 88
relationship problems and, 114
Relapsing diseases, 53
Relationship problems, 114, 115
Residential treatment, 77, 91
Return-to-work strategy, 101
Right to vote, 155
Risk reduction, 80
Rite of passage, 34, 36
Road Rules (TV program), 147
Russ C. (addict), 28–30

S
Safe work environment, 150
Safety-sensitive workforce, 44
SAMHSA (Substance Abuse
and Mental Health Services
Administration), 20, 25, 85, 101,
126
Sample, Barry, 45
Saner, Emine, 73–77
Satel, Sally, 57–61
Saying no, 118
SBIRT (screening brief interven-
tion and referral to treatment)
momentum for, 122–23
statistics, 124–25
trends, 123–25, 127